Robertson Davies (1913–   )

JOHN MILLS

Robertson Davies (1913–   )

JOHN MILLS

Biography

ROBERTSON DAVIES was born on 28 August 1913 in Thamesville, Ontario, the son of William Rupert Davies, publisher of the Thamesville *Herald* and later a senator, and his wife, Florence (Mackay). Davies grew up in relatively affluent circumstances and was educated accordingly: at Upper Canada College, and later, Queen's University in Kingston — a city which he disguised as "Salterton" and which forms the locale of his first two novels. Davies' inability to cope with mathematics led him to be admitted to Queen's as a "special student," a course which did not, however, lead to a degree. After three years at Queen's, Davies went on to Oxford, where he received a B.Litt. in 1938, writing, as his thesis, a study of Shakespeare's boy actors.

During his residence at Oxford, Davies was a stage manager for the Oxford University Drama Society. Later he toured the English provinces with an acting company and then worked for a year for the Old Vic Repertory Company, where one of his colleagues was Tyrone Guthrie — a founder, in postwar years, of the Stratford Festival. He returned to Canada in 1940 to become literary editor of *Saturday Night* and, in 1942, editor of the *Peterborough Examiner*. In 1960 he began teaching English at the University of Toronto and was appointed first Master of Massey College in 1962.

Davies started his career as an actor and producer of plays and began writing his own plays during the 1940s. By the end of that decade, he had established himself as a dramatist and essayist — two collections of articles for the *Peterborough Examiner*, written by his alter ego, "Samuel Marchbanks," appeared during 1947–49, as well as the plays *Overlaid*, *Eros at Breakfast*, and *Fortune, My Foe*. He published three novels during the

1950s (*Tempest-Tost, Leaven of Malice,* and *A Mixture of Frail-ties*), three plays (*At My Heart's Core, A Masque of Aesop,* and *A Jig for the Gypsy*), and innumerable articles, reviews, and essays. During this period, he found the time to serve on the board of governors of the Stratford Festival, an experience which informs the unpromisingly titled *Twice Have the Trumpets Sounded* and *Thrice the Brinded Cat Hath Mew'd,* accounts of the festival for 1954 and 1955 respectively, both written in collabo-ration with Tyrone Guthrie. Teaching, journalism, and academic administration kept Davies busy for a number of years, and he did not publish another novel until *Fifth Business* appeared in 1970. *The Manticore* and *World of Wonders* followed within five years, and in 1981, Davies published his seventh novel, *The Rebel Angels.*

Honours and awards have come early and easily to Robertson Davies, and in many respects he seems an "establishment" figure, by which I mean that his family background is middle-class and wealthy, his schooling very nearly impeccable, and the number of honorary degrees to his name prodigious. These include degrees from McMaster, Bishops, and McGill universities, from the universities of Windsor, Manitoba, and Western Ontario, and many more. He was made a Fellow of the Royal Society of Canada in 1967, and a Companion of the Order of Canada in 1972. He has won the Stephen Leacock Medal for Humour for *Leaven of Malice,* and the Governor General's Award for *The Manticore.* The posts and honours accorded him have placed him at the very top of his nation's cultural life, and at the same time, he is admired internationally, certainly as a novelist.

Yet it is by no means possible to categorize Davies' work as "establishment," whatever one may say about its creator. It is singularly "unstuffy" and colloquial; and thematically it supports values which can be characterized as liberal, including a rejection of small-town narrowness, criticism of the family, and a commit-ment to self-evaluation and personal growth. His presence in our literature is somehow, even after we have looked closely at indi-vidual works, greater than the sum of its parts, and his influence has been a good one — on the side of the "Eros men," as a char-acter in his *A Mixture of Frailties* puts it, as opposed to the followers of Thanatos.

Tradition and Milieu

When we consider the developments and experiments that have gone on in the arenas of fiction and theatre alone during the eighty-odd years of this century, we could be forgiven for supposing that there has never been an era of equivalent artistic ferment. Fiction, for instance, moved away from the nineteenth-century, three-decker, basically frivolous entertainment intended to provide a blend of representationalism and romance towards an increasing concern for realism and moral weight. Such writers as Henry James made readers much more aware of the dialogue that exists between reader and writer, of the intense illusions of reality that could be obtained by shifts in "angle of narration," of the inveigling manipulations inherent in the dramatization of narrative and the comparative elimination of the authorial voice. Other novelists such as Zola, ascribing sociological and political dimensions to the novel, spoke of a scientific fiction which would examine conditions in societies much as would a scientist, and asserted that the purpose of art is to bring about, or facilitate, social change. Other writers and theoreticians strove for a greater "realism" in their descriptions of human beings not only by delineating outward behaviour more accurately but also by taking account of thought processes and the newly named Unconscious (personal, collective, or other) and by inventing techniques for their inclusion such as stream of consciousness, surrealism, expressionism, Vorticism, and so on. This is "modernism," and it has been rendered obsolete, or so it might seem, by "post-modernism," which considers fiction in terms of symbol, pattern, artifice, instead of plot, character, setting. None of this ferment seems to have affected Robertson Davies. Though he uses Jungian concepts to structure his fictional characters, his novels are conventional in form and genre. He is totally uninterested in precipitating social change, though much of his work is mildly edged with satire, nor does his writing seek to convince its readers by its solemnity. In many respects this is refreshing. Davies clearly belongs to a reactionary camp in these matters, but it is as though formalism and the general question of "form" hold no interest for him and that what he has to say can best be said only in the traditional manner. Thus it is hard to speak of influence on his work in any contemporary sense: his influences seem rather to be Trollope, Waugh, Cary, Peacock, Shaw, Butler, Leacock, and so on — writers whose vision of human life is basically comic, and about many of whom Davies has written wisely.

A similar brief account of the theatre in our century shows a development from the well-made play presented by fourth-wall illusionists, to the Shavian drama of ideas, to the incorporation of "modernism" on the stage with corresponding changes in theatrical techniques resulting from the experiments of men like Brecht, Piscator, and Artaud. When I think of the last couple of decades, such catch phrases as Epic Theatre, Theatre of the Absurd, Theatre of Cruelty, Living Theatre, Comedy of Menace, and several more come to mind. Davies, again, seems not to have been influenced in his stage work by any of these "movements," except in so far as he pokes mild fun at them in his plays generally and, particularly, in his "masques."

The other event in the last few years that has crept into our specifically Canadian consciousnesses is the development of literary nationalism. It is not part of my intention to provide a capsule history of this, or any other, literary movement, but it is necessary to state that it exists as a half-heard continuo in much Canadian writing, was resuscitated as a major theme by Northrop Frye, and given popular expression by Margaret Atwood in her seminal book *Survival*. Davies is more affected by such nationalism than would at first glance appear. Much dramatic energy in the early plays, for instance, depends upon the conflict between what Davies perceives as Canadian small-town values — work, duty, moral earnestness, piety — and delight, art, joy, freedom, and life affirmation. Some of this work for the theatre is didactic, even though one message Davies seems concerned to communicate is that art is not for messages. Yet the tenor of his first plays is fairly clear — it is an attempt to present "Eros" to his audiences and enlist them against the forces of "Thanatos." In *Fortune, My Foe*, the problem is posed as one of patriotism: is it right to pursue life, liberty, and art in countries such as the United States or Britain, where such things are valued, or to stay in Canada and try to work with the refractory material at hand? Nicholas, the play's hero, opts to remain in Canada on the grounds that if every man or woman of talent ran away, the country could never improve. Davies takes up this issue again in *A Mixture of Frailties* with regard to its heroine, Monica Gall, a promising opera singer whose upbringing in the Canadian city of Salterton is said to be culturally under-nourished. Much of Davies' own patriotism is directed satirically against the men and women who, he thinks, will consciously or unconsciously hold Canada back from achieving its rightful place as a country of artistic maturity capable of nourishing its citizens spiritually as well as materially. In the later Deptford trilogy, it takes a more defensive form, where it exists at all. It is as though he is claiming that such men as Dunstan Ramsay, Magnus Eisengrim, Percy and David Staunton—outwardly dull and conformist and thus in accordance with the Canadian stereotype—are still living lives of as great an interest to analysts, policemen, and priests as they would be were they lived by Rimbaud, say, or some equally colourful non-Canadian. Davies has not, so far as I can tell, been much affected by the now unfashionable thematic criticism of Canadian literature, which has attempted to prescribe what the Canadian novelist and poet should write about. This is vastly to his credit, as is the catho-licity of his reading tastes, and his sanity concerning the preva-lent notion that Canadians should read Canadian books, even the third-rate ones, before they read the world masterpieces.

Critical Overview and Context

Davies was treated seriously as a writer at the very start of his career. The reviews of his first book, *Shakespeare's Boy Actors*, were in general favourable: it was described as an "able and interesting but very uneven piece of work" by *The Times Literary Supplement*, which also considered, significantly enough, that Davies was at his best when examining the comedies;[1] *The Quarterly Review* described it as "judicious and admirable in its style and suggestions."[2] *The Diary of Samuel Marchbanks* was praised very highly as "some of the brightest humour and most vigorous satire produced by a Canadian"[3] and as a rival to *Sunshine Sketches of a Little Town*.[4] The play *Fortune, My Foe* was less well received. Its "bright talk" was found to be mainly confined to "questionable and unilluminating generalities,"[5] its characters, to be "wooden" and "irritating caricatures,"[6] and the entire play, "faintly reminiscent of Shaw both in its talky nature and in its wit."[7] Davies redeemed himself among the reviewers with his second Marchbanks book, which *The Times Literary Supplement* praised for its "warm and witty humanism,"[8] and with the plays contained in *Eros at Breakfast and Other Plays* and *At My Heart's Core*, variously characterized as "colourful, gay, and quite indescribable"[9] (presumably a compliment) and "wise and witty";[10] Davies himself was called "by far the most competent literary craftsman currently operating in Canada."[11]

Davies' first novel, *Tempest-Tost*, was greeted in this country with enthusiasm. In an extravagantly worded review, the *Toronto Daily Star* claimed that it was an "exercise in puckish persiflage studded with shrewd apercus and witty aphorisms and tricked out in esoteric and sometimes epicene dialogue."[12] *Saturday Night* hailed the author as "the Canadian Smollett" in his tendency towards caricature and breeziness of style,[13] while Davies' rendition of a small Ontario town put another reviewer in mind of Sinclair Lewis; the same reviewer found the novel as a whole comparable to the best works of its kind in England and the United States.[14] Claude Bissell thought that the novel was a "refreshing departure from the studied realism that so far has characterized [Canada's] best fiction."[15] Foreign opinion was less amiable: *The Manchester Guardian* did not like the novel very much;[16] *The Times Literary Supplement* damned it faintly as a "pleasant little farce" that "would not be out of place in the setting of an English village";[17] while *The New York Times Book Review* hinted that the novel would have been greatly improved had the spirit of Angela Thirkell been given a freer play.[18] *Leaven of Malice*, the second Salterton book, was found to be "lightweight...but amusing,"[19] "witty and urbane" ("reflecting the wide erudition and observation of the author"),[20] and a comedy of manners (as opposed to a comedy of "life").[21] Claude Bissell described it as "within the tradition of E.M. Forster and most of the Victorians," except that the novel "has no real protagonist: the hero of the book is the gay, disinterested mind."[22] John Metcalf, in the *Spectator*, praised its professional smoothness and noted the novel's "curiously nineteenth-century feel...as though *Leaven of Malice* was a poor Canadian's *Middlemarch*";[23] while an anonymous reviewer in *The New*

Yorker pointed to what I believe is a major flaw in Davies' work: "Salterton is a diverting place, and Mr. Davies is a clever writer, but his characters don't seem to be sunk quite deeply enough in hypocrisy or any other evil to deserve the sharpness of the attack he launches against them."[24] This is a criticism to which I shall return later in my essay.

A Mixture of Frailties, the last of the Salterton novels, was generally regarded as a step forward in Davies' growth as a novelist. Trollope, not Smollett, was invoked this time,[25] while Davies' characters were believed to be "real red-blooded people" who "live and breathe, and love and hate, and make all kinds of foolish mistakes."[26] Arnold Edinborough claimed that *Mixture* is an "adult novel" (whatever that may mean) rooted in the traditions of Dickens and George Eliot,[27] and Claude Bissell, with some reservations, greeted it as Davies' "first serious novel."[28] *The New Yorker* disagreed: "The book belongs to the school of fiction that derives from Trollope by way of Angela Thirkell.... In an odd way, it manages to be readable and amusing without being very interesting."[29]

The so-called Deptford trilogy has established Davies' reputation both in Canada and abroad as a major novelist. During the twelve-year period between the publication of *A Mixture of Frailties* and *Fifth Business,* he published his book of essays *A Voice from the Attic*, a toned-down Marchbanks volume filled with wise saw, modern instance, humanity, and wit. Its reception varied from Max Cosman's positive opinion that it is the "literate, the colloquial, the discursive yet patterned table talk of one who is sensible of human nature's ordinariness and the need to raise it above itself,"[30] to Kerry McSweeney's negative view that *Attic* confirms both Davies' "exceptionally lucid and vigorous prose" and his shallow point of view: "...there is no real intellectual depth..., no social vision, and far too much indulgence of his fondness for the second-rate and the trivial."[31] I believe this to be a valid position with regard to Davies' work, though I would like, in succeeding pages, to make some modifications to it.

Fifth Business was almost universally praised — "profound, erudite, vigorous," raved *The Montreal Star*,[32] while *The New York Times* described it as "a marvellously enigmatic novel,... elegantly written and driven by irresistible narrative force."[33] A reviewer in *Book World* even went so far as to claim it as a work of "theological fiction that approaches Graham Greene at the top of his form."[34] *The Manticore* received notices almost as enthusiastic, and what dissent there was generally hinged on the problem of whether the novel could be read separately from the first or not. But Davies' reputation was, by this time, such that attacks on him, or even mild reservations regarding his work, had become within the range of the "unthinkable." Thus *World of Wonders*, which concludes the Deptford trilogy, was regarded as a major novelistic achievement despite the fact, and I hope to demonstrate that it *is* a fact, that *World of Wonders* and its immediate predecessors are seriously flawed novels, in regard to both structure and theme. Perhaps the most enthusiastic statement came from the prestigious magazine *Newsweek*: "... Davies' trilogy is one of the splendid literary enterprises of this decade." *Fifth Business* "is the most haunting"; the second novel is "remarkable." *World of Wonders* is "the most richly textured of the three" and deeper than it seems. Having lost "Spengler's 'Magian World View,'" and its sense of unfathomable wonder, "we must be grateful" for "Robertson Davies educating us right back into it again."[35]

The reader wading through this ephemeral and instant criticism may be forgiven for supposing that the consensus regarding Davies' oeuvre is similar to what Chesterton once said concerning the voluminous works of H. G. Wells: "reading him is like standing on the edge of a mighty, limitless ocean — one quarter of an inch deep." What the book reviewers and the literate public made of Davies up until the first scholarly articles on *Fifth Business* began to appear could quite fairly be paraphrased as follows: he is a witty, urbane, wise, puckish writer who has taken on the mantle of men like Leacock (whom he rivals) or even Shaw (to whom he is inferior) and who is busy creating a body of entertaining but ultimately lightweight fiction. The mind of a book reviewer (and I am one myself) thrives on comparisons and contrasts of this sort, for they save him the work of elucidating what it is in a given writer's work that makes it unique and idiosyncratic. Yet the growing enthusiasm for the Deptford trilogy among the reviewers resulted in Davies being taken up by the more academic and scholarly critics, who tend to consider the novels and plays in groups, tracing themes

8

and motifs and creating overviews. Ivon Owen's article "The Salterton Novels," published in *The Tamarack Review*, is an early example of a good essay of this type. Owen perceives the recurrent theme in the Salterton trilogy to be the Freudian one of the "possessive parent and the too-compliant child":[36] the theme darkens in *Leaven of Malice*, and is contrapuntally interwoven in *A Mixture of Frailties* with a motif concerning the interdependence of "art-and-life." Owen also notes that Davies "stands curiously apart from the main stream of contemporary fiction."[37] Davies' contribution to the art of satire is examined by Hugo McPherson in another interesting and capable essay, which asserts that behind the mask of satirist there lives "a serious writer of romance" concerned mostly with the plight of the imagination in a cultural wasteland.[38] Davies' Marchbanks was created in an early attempt to fight "the glum sobriety of Calvinism" (p. 164), but he never comes alive as a character. The narratorial persona in *Tempest-Tost* is no more than a "disembodied voice" (p. 166). Only in *A Mixture of Frailties* does Davies create the balance of romance and satire he has been seeking, and, in the heroine's education, he has also created a sort of metaphor for the liberation of the Canadian imagination from "second-rateness, parochialism and dullness" (pp. 172–73). In a later article, McPherson is concerned with something he calls "the discovery of self" and with the notion that the Salterton trilogy presents the failures and victories of the "imagination" to free itself.[39]

Davies' debt to Aldous Huxley and Evelyn Waugh is examined by Desmond Pacey, who claims that the application of the British writers' serio-comic techniques to Canadian themes resulted in fresh and exciting work.[40] Like most other critics, Pacey observes a progression from apprenticeship to comparative mastery in the course of the early trilogy.

The second trilogy has invited considerable involvement with the theories of Jung — partly because of what Davies has said in print about Jung's influence on him but mostly, of course, because of the novel's specifically Jungian content: *The Manticore*, in fact, is a blow-by-blow description of a Jungian analysis. Gordon Roper has written a pioneering précis of this influence and provided a concise, if simplified, account of Jung's theories of psychology and myth, linking them to the protagonist's search for psychic wholeness in *Fifth Business*.[41] Yet another, though closely linked, dimension is Davies' exploration of the interconnections among the magical and the real, the logical and rational and the inexplicable.[42]

Up to the present time, four books have appeared on Robertson Davies. Judith Skelton Grant's short monograph in the New Canadian Library series on Canadian writers serves as an introduction to the biographical facts of Davies' life and of his involvement with the stage.[43] Her discussion of the novels is less satisfactory since her critical approach is not clearly stated and a couple of key ideas are offered rather too tentatively. One is the distinction she makes between "significant" and "organizing" action, and the other concerns Davies' use of framing devices: both concepts are interesting, but Grant is unable, for reasons of space, to develop them.

Studies in Robertson Davies' Deptford Trilogy, edited by Robert G. Lawrence and Samuel L. Macey, is much more specialized and singles out, in a series of individual essays, a number of issues, some of them minor, in Davies' later work. These essays range from the illuminating (F. L. Radford's on the Salterton trilogy and on the Jungian concept of the Great Mother), through the playful (Patricia Merivale's tracing of affinities with Hugh MacLennan, Scott Fitzgerald, Conrad, Nabokov — almost everybody, in fact — interspersed with wise remarks on "elegiac romance"), to the ingenious (Macey's "Time, Clockwork, and the Devil in Robertson Davies' Deptford Trilogy"). The best and worst features of academic criticism manifest themselves in this book: there are essays, such as Radford's, which both challenge the reader and encourage him in his own investigations; there are others which communicate the air of the graduate student's carrel — smelling dankly of chalk-dust and ink-horn; and others contain magisterial statements like "...through [Davies'] sometimes certain and sometimes faltering analysis of the development of [his major characters] he increases the reader's awareness of the proper relationship that should exist between public and private selves,"[44] which suggests a level of consciousness and judgement superior to that of the novelist himself, but not obviously demonstrated in the main body of the essay.

The best of the four books for the general reader is, in my

opinion, Elspeth Buitenhuis' volume in Forum House's Canadian Writers and Their Works series, despite the fact that its publication preceded the last two volumes of the Deptford trilogy.[45] It serves, however, as a useful introduction to Davies' early work, to which Buitenhuis is engagingly sympathetic, though she also subscribes to the conventional wisdom that the first three books are promising apprenticework leading to the fulfilment of *Fifth Business*. She makes an interesting attempt to show that a central episode in *Leaven of Malice* is a metaphor for that novel's structure, which, in turn, can be described as "balanced" and "classical" — words that call for more definition than Buitenhuis is able to give them. She sees Davies as the creator of "satiric romance" — a category of Northrop Frye's wherein romance features as the quest of some hero figure for a precious object ("wisdom" in the case of *Fifth Business*), and satire, as the undermining of the pretentions of the romance. Thus the genre walks an emotional tightrope: The Marchbanks persona, for instance, is both classically antiromantic and Dionysian — flirting, as Marchbanks seems to, with romantic attachments to anarchy and chaos. There is a sense, she claims, in Davies' work of powerful Dionysian forces, whose upsurge is checked and harnessed by social law. In this, she asserts, following Frye, he is typical of his "garrison" culture.

Patricia Monk's *The Smaller Infinity: The Jungian Self in the Novels of Robertson Davies* was published too late for me to include a full discussion of it in this essay. As its title suggests, however, it attempts to trace the affinity, defined here as spiritual attraction, between Jung's writings and Davies' fiction. Monk is interested in dualities, or what another sort of critic might call binary oppositions, such as transcendence / mundaneness, actuality / appearance, microcosm / macrocosm, and she tries, I think successfully, to establish a link between Jung's concept of human identity and Davies' theme of personal liberation. Again, this book is for the specialist interested in a strictly psychological approach to literature.

It seems to me that the Jungian and Freudian elements in Davies' fiction have now been profitably and properly examined, and to persist in a study of them would be to take the author at his own evaluation and to engage him where he is most weak. Buitenhuis' book implicitly suggests lines of approach the would-be critic or student could now pursue. What does it mean, for example, to describe Davies as a "satirist"? Or as a "romantic"? What are the shapes, the structures, of his novels and plays? In addition, work needs to be done on Davies' narrators, on the novels as varieties of *performance*, or as versions, to use a word from Russian formalist criticism, of *skaz*, and of the language and shifting intonations and modulations of the *skazochnik* himself.

Davies' Works

As a critic attempting an evaluation of Robertson Davies' prodigious output, I am confronted with plays, essays, journalism, facetiae, novels, criticism, books on Shakespeare, books on Stratford, collections of editorials written in the persona of Samuel Marchbanks, book reviews, epigrams, sententious utterances, and so on. If I try to deal with it all, I cannot avoid being superficial; if I concentrate on a small part of it, I shall be accused of narrowness. I will nevertheless choose the latter course and risk being both narrow and superficial, and I choose it for a number of reasons. First, I am not competent to make judgements on Davies' theatre work. I have seen none of it performed and would thus have to treat each play as though it were a kind of prose fiction. As prose fictions, the plays seem to me unsatisfactory, though I have no doubt that they work well enough on the stage. Fortunately I can refer the reader to Patricia Morley's book on Robertson Davies in the Profiles in Canadian Drama series.[46] It is an adequate introduction to the plays, though somewhat marred by plot summary included at the expense of analysis. Secondly, the Marchbanks table-talk volumes are entertaining but, taken on their own, ephemeral. They are mildly amusing exercises in curmudgeonmanship and do not require the block-and-tackle effort of the literary critic to disentangle. Finally, Davies' essays, speeches, and occasional writings appear to me equally ephemeral in interest, though readable and often elegantly written. I would like, then, to assert plainly what I feel to be obvious: that Davies' best work appears in his seven novels; that these are what literary people associate with his name; that the novels form the basis for his international reputation; and that, were it not for the existence of these novels, he would be a minor, and only moderately interesting, literary figure. Furthermore, there is considerable critical commentary on the second trilogy and not much on the first. I will therefore concentrate most of my attention on the first trilogy.

In style and substance, the Deptford trilogy develops from the earlier Salterton novels, which seem to me underrated. *Tempest-Tost*, *Leaven of Malice*, and *A Mixture of Frailties* are generally more successful books than their less conventional successors since their genesis lies more in the desire to entertain than to instruct. Davies' sententiousness riddles them throughout, just as it does the Deptford trilogy, but in the earlier novels it is more controlled, and subordinated to the demands of narrative and characterization. I would like to examine *Tempest-Tost*, particularly its first chapter, in some detail because I think this is where Davies' strengths and weaknesses as a novelist emerge very clearly, and where his main theme, that of personal liberation, is first encountered.

There is, generally, no sense of specific time in the first trilogy, nor any sense of place outside Salterton in its first two novels. Thus the action of the books could take place at any time from about 1925 onwards. The novels resemble in form, structure, and atmosphere the work of certain minor English novelists, particularly detective-story writers like Margery Allingham or Nicholas Blake (Cecil Day Lewis), though the latter's occasional use of imaginative language seems beyond Davies. There is similar unreality of place and time, the same affable, foible-conscious narrator, and the same lack of fictional substance — by which I mean that the imaginative realm to which I, the reader, can assent and which is either plausible in terms of character, plot, psychological motivation, and setting, as in the traditional novel, or in terms of image, pattern, and symbol as in "experimental" fiction, has not been created.

The action of *Tempest-Tost* concerns the struggles of a group of people to mount a production of *The Tempest* in the Ontario town of Salterton, their intrigues, and the relationships existing among them. It is in no sense a picture of a small Canadian city — and here Davies may have missed an opportunity to satisfy the voracious Canadian appetite for representationalism — because the field of action is too narrow and its main characters (academics, teachers, professional men and women, the sons and daughters of wealthy businessmen) share the same social values.

The opening chapter presents most of the novel's characters: Mr. Webster, whose large garden is to be used for the production; his two daughters, Fredegonde and Griselda; Professor Vambrace and Nellie Forrester, members of the Little Theatre Committee; its treasurer, Hector Mackilwraith; a university instructor named Solomon (Solly) Bridgetower and his mother; a director, Valentine Rich, brought in to work on the play; and a couple of minor characters, such as the one with whom the novel starts, Tom Gwalchmai, Mr. Webster's gardener. Davies' Fieldingesque narratorial persona is also presented, and it does not change appreciably over the two trilogies, whether rendered in the third-person, unashamedly omniscient and intrusive, mode, or in the first-person, as in the Deptford trilogy. This narrator's habit is to sidetrack the drama of the plot to deliver to the reader little essays, snippets of folk wisdom, homilies, and comments on the human condition. Though these comments are often banal, their thrust is usually mild and genial. The following comment regarding Mr. Webster is an example:

> He was, it was argued, "in a position to entertain"; most of the people who "gave of their time and effort" in order to advance causes "were not in a position to entertain"; the least that he could do to minimize the offence of being better off than these good people was to assume the entertaining position upon demand. But he did not like to have other people taking their pleasure with his gardens any more than he would have liked to have other people take their pleasure with his wife, if that lady had been living.[47]

This passage seems to me characteristic of Davies' narrative stance and technique. The phrase "it was argued" is purposefully blank and suggests small, tightly knit gossip schools where such matters as "positions" are argued because, other than social responsibilities and the precise location of other people on the social spectrum, there is little else to discuss. The topics argued focus on "entertaining," a word which, because of its context, conveys less of the orgiastic than it does the stuffed-shirt ritual. The "offence" of being better-off than these "good" people is not Davies coming down on the side of the rich — but it is not precisely Webster's thought process either. Instead it is the trope of a man affectionately observing the foibles of his own milieu; the people, because they feel offended at the existence of somebody richer than they, can be described as "good" only by a gentle ironist, and this is the effect that Davies seems to be striving for. The last sentence contains the seed of a good epigram, but its phrasing is so flat-footed that it suggests more the attempts of an elephant to dance on a trampoline than it does the elegant sword-thrust of wit. And it is at this point that it is necessary to comment on Davies' style.

Whatever else Davies is read for, it cannot be for the felicity of his prose. It is rarely more than adequate; more often it is halting, pedestrian, unmetaphorical, and journalistic, qualities which this passage, selected at random from the second chapter of *Tempest-Tost*, will serve to illustrate:

> "It had occurred to me that I might try my hand at Gonzalo. The wise old counsellor," said Hector, looking around for appreciation of this joke. But there was none. Professor Vambrace felt that in some way he had been finessed, and was trying to figure out where; Nellie was wondering if she had not been wrong, half an hour ago, to feel so warmly toward Hector; why, the man was nothing but a self-seeker and his obvious counting on her support seemed, in some inexplicable way, to dim the brightness of Mrs. Caesar Augustus Conquergood. Valentine Rich and Solly had made up their minds independently that it was plain that, whoever cast the play, they were not to be allowed to do it. The gathering had a somewhat stunned and inward-looking air as it ate the sticky buns and coffee which Nellie brought forth, aided by the faithful Roscoe. (p. 59)

Why is Hector's remark "a joke"? There is a sense in which he does indeed see himself as a wise old counsellor — if such a description is a joke when expressed to others, it becomes an attempt at ironic self-deprecation totally out-of-character. It is not clear, however, whether Davies is "inside" Hector's head at this point. If he is not, then the narrator is seeing the "joke," in which case he is simply feebleminded. The sentence beginning "Professor Vambrace" is incoherent for similar reasons: "in some way" is vague and out-of-character since a man priding himself on classical brevity would express himself precisely, or, if that is not necessarily the case in "real life," it is certainly in accordance with the stereotyped classics don that Davies is trying to create. *Why* does Vambrace feel finessed? "Trying to figure out" is an unimpressive colloquialism, particularly when applied to this character, and the entire sentence suggests the end of a hard day experienced by a man paid at so much a word. In the next passage, beginning "Nellie," the narrator attempts to get inside the head of Nellie Forrester, who seems, with her "in some inexplicable way," as vague as the professor. "That it was plain that" is a phrase in which we once again hear the elephant on the trampoline; the auxiliary verb "had" in the last sentence communicates a sloppiness customary when used in place of a real verb; while the slyly portentous "Nellie brought forth," contrasted with the triviality of the sticky buns, results in the cuteness of diluted mock-epic and in a narratorial, mechanical smirk.

I have no wish to attack Davies' style in detail—indeed, almost every writer is vulnerable to this sort of analysis. It is necessary, however, to establish what Davies is *not* before we decide what he *is*. The amateurishness of the novel also affects the structure of the first chapter in the scene between Fredegonde and Tom Gwalchmai, who are as close friends as it is possible to be for a fourteen-year-old girl of middle-class background, with the tastes — High Anglicanism and oenology — to go with it, and a gardener employed full-time by her father. Davies spends much energy delineating this couple but is unable to do much with them once they are introduced — they appear in the subsequent action in the most minor of roles. The point of the scene is to establish the basic plot and to introduce other characters through "reliable" perceptions.

There follows a portrayal of Salterton, a thriving city with a cathedral, a military college, a university, and pretensions to historic importance. Once again, the amusing, fluently delivered material leads nowhere—the city does not reappear in the novel and is irrelevant to the narrative. It is neither in itself a character, as in Dickens, nor does it play any part in the formation of the novel's personalities. The description exists purely as a separable essay. Tom Gwalchmai's toolshed is featured next and there is a further expenditure of energy on the rendering of this immaculate and precious bailiwick. The shed is perhaps not quite as irrelevant as Salterton in the novel, for Hector Mackilwraith makes his clumsy attempt at suicide within it, but there seems no psychological or iconological reason why this shed should be so lavishly described.

Members of the Little Theatre group invade the shed, and severally they betray forms of affectation and *mauvaise foi*. Mrs. Forrester, for instance, addresses Fredegonde:

> "You'll be Freddy," said Mrs. Forrester, who liked to use the Gaelic form of assertion jocosely. She was not a Scot herself, but she liked to enrich her conversation with what she believed to be Scottish and Irish idioms. "How sweet you look, sitting there with your wee bookie!" (p. 18)

Marred though the passage is with tautology and repetition, the label Davies gives her is pleasant enough. Similarly:

> Professor Vambrace gave what he doubtless meant to be a friendly glance, but was really a baleful glare, at both Tom and Freddy, to be shared between them.
> "Wet," said he. Classics was his subject, and he sometimes affected a classical simplicity in social conversation. (pp. 18–19)

And again, when Solly Bridgetower, a young instructor at Waverley University, describes Hector as a "creaking pedant," he feels compelled to explain the phrase:

> "I speak, of course, in a rich, Elizabethan manner," said Solly, with a rich, Elizabethan gesture which almost toppled a tower of small flower pots. (p. 20)

These affectations are recognizable as varieties of personae with which we all confront the world and each other, and they are probably worth poking mild fun at. The narrator himself is by no means devoid of such affectations: he comes over as "the amiable old buffer" with a wicked eye for pretension; as a mild-mannered nineteenth-century essayist nudging the reader and winking at him, but up-to-date in diction; in short, as a combination of Pecksniff and Elia, but disguised as a bearded uncle self-consciously on the side of youth against the pomposities and self-deceptions of middle age. The labels he attaches to his characters in the shed do not, however, stick. Solly becomes much more sympathetic as the novel progresses, and his Elizabethan mannerisms are transferred to Humphrey Cobbler — the most vivid, the best-realized, character in the trilogy. Davies seems to forget about Nellie's pseudo-Scottishness and the professor's brevity as his creations begin to grow away from his first perceptions of them.

The shed scene ends with a well-described row between Solly and Mrs. Forrester, and Davies' mild irony sharpens somewhat when he describes the latter's emotions:

> Mrs. Forrester never lost her temper. She prided herself upon this trait and frequently mentioned it to her friends. But sometimes, as upon the present occasion, she felt a burning in the pit of her stomach which would have been anger in anyone else. How stupid it was of Solly not to be able to take a rebuke without all this bickering. (p. 22)

Almost as deadly is his description of her "pout which had been rather attractive fifteen years earlier" (pp. 25–26), and devastating in intention if not quite in execution is the passage on the Forresters' "Taste" in interior design and their predilection for mushroom tints, colours suggestive of vomit, and chairs with no arms sitting on a "spring-like arrangement of bent wood" which was "very modern indeed, and avoided by all save the lightest guests" (p. 27).

In contrast to the less substantial Forresters, Mr. Webster likes heavy things made from solid wood, Persian carpets, leather upholstery, panelling, and so on — an old-money Edwardian clubman taste. He is obviously intended to be a sympathetic figure despite, or perhaps because of, his unashamed conventionality. He is mild-mannered, unpretentious, and, as a widower, insecure only as to the correct handling of his daughters as they grow into womanhood. Fredegonde Webster is also held up to the reader's admiration: she is sharp and perceptive and does not suffer fools, like Nellie Forrester, gladly. Her sparse room contains both a crucifix and a print of Poussin's *The Feeding of the Infant Bacchus*, which reflect her two interests and create a pleasant, apparent incongruity between the Christian and pagan worlds Freddy inhabits. She observes, at bedtime, her thin but developing body in the mirror and compares it, unfavourably, to her sister's.

Griselda also prepares for bed, and Davies contrasts her quite neatly with the ascetic Freddy by describing the luxurious bath in which she wallows, smoking cigarettes and eating chocolates. The incongruity associated with *her*— and repetition of the trick renders it slightly mechanical — lies in her taste for literature which includes the innocently ribald works of writers like Thorne Smith with the novels of Trollope.

From this comfortable household with its various inhabitants at comparative peace with themselves and the world, Davies moves to a greasy spoon called the Snak Shak, where Hector Mackilwraith sits amid the plastic decor, neon lighting, and jukeboxes. Over a less than pretentious meal, he works out the advantages and disadvantages concerning asking for a role in *The Tempest* production by dividing a page of paper into two columns and systematically writing them down. This methodical approach to life's problems is Hector's "humour," though, as in the case of the other characters in the novels, Davies' creation refuses to be limited to the boundaries his "humour" suggests.

In the next section, Davies describes the Bridgetower household and shows us Solly's mother unflatteringly as a woman whose bald spot "glow[s] dustily" (p. 41) in the light of an ugly, though grand and solemn, lamp suspended from the ceiling by a rusty chain. The lampshade is made of glass strips, coloured green and yellow and flecked with red—a lampshade resembling "vitrified mucous" (p. 41). This lamp, fashionable in its day, is an objectification of Mrs. Bridgetower's considerable, but wasted and distorted, intellect, which nurtures itself not only on what Saint Paul calls *kakoethia*, a form of malignancy in which all human actions are perceived as basely motivated, but on outmoded expressions of paranoid xenophobia — for example, her concern about the "Yellow Peril" (p. 42). Another image expressing the psychic health of the Bridgetower *ménage* is the cabinet with leaded glass windows, in which the ceremonial china, never to be used, is imprisoned.

Similarly imprisoning is the formal way of life Mrs. Bridgetower adopts with Solly based on British middle-class customs as perceived by a colonial consciousness. Solly is encased in a dark coat, for instance, whenever he dines with her; the conversation between them on these occasions must be "suitable"; and the fiction that he, as a male, must be left alone to enjoy his port before he joins her for coffee is maintained. It is with Mrs. Bridgetower that Solly discusses the play and its cast, though the conversation consists of assertion by himself and denigratory responses from his mother applied particularly to any girls involved to whom she thinks he might be attracted. They retire to "a gloomy drawing-room, where a great many books lived in glass and leaden prisons, like the china in the dining-room" (p. 45).

Solly, alone at last in his bedroom, wishes he possessed the courage to phone Griselda. A sense of impotence, growing from a fear of his mother, saddens him; his courtship of Griselda is subsequently inhibited by his sense of Mrs. Bridgetower's displeasure, which issued "from her rather as the haze of ecto-plasm issues from a spiritualist medium, [and] filled the house whenever he came home late" (p. 68). Her ill health and vulnera-bility enchain him — he is her servant and just as much her pris-oner as the books and china behind their walls of glass and lead. Solly loses Griselda, and, in this novel, does not succeed in escaping. Yet, unlike Hector, he is aware of his imprisonment:

> He needed freedom. He needed a profession at which he could support himself. He needed the love and reassurance of someone other than his mother. He needed someone to whom he could talk, without reserve, about the humiliating thralldom which she had imposed on him since his thir-teenth year. As he sat in his armchair, sipping his miserable drink, a few stinging tears of self-pity mounted to his eyes. Self-pity is commonly held to be despicable; it can also be a great comfort if it does not become chronic. (p. 126)

This, though marred by the last sentence (a spurious profun-dity so carefully hedged as to be meaningless), is still eloquent enough and expresses Davies' sense that one's major liberationist acts must be first directed against one's parents. In fact, this is the chief theme of Davies' writing. It is announced in *Tempest-Tost*, particularly in the first three chapters, and developed slightly in the other Salterton novels. Solly, Hector, and Pearl Vambrace, the professor's daughter, are the prisoners in this first novel, and each is conscious in various degrees and at different times of the need to struggle towards freedom. Davies is particularly good at showing how Pearl "awakens" to her enslavement, and how Hector, having won a number of vital battles, believes that he has freed himself. Both, consciously or unconsciously, seek freedom, and both regard *The Tempest* production, with the heightened emotional intensity surrounding the theatre generally and this play, with its symbols of magic and liberation, in particular, as the catalyst for their escape—as though, mundane inhabitants of a colonial backwater, they could yet become engulfed in a mystery that will set them free.

Though it includes much that is structurally irrelevant, the first chapter of *Tempest-Tost* is a busy and entertaining one, and it ends with an apt yet surprising image of Valentine Rich, the play's director, mourning for her grandfather and the "necessary death of the well-loved, wise old man" (p. 47). Davies has succeeded in establishing his characters, one-dimensional though they may be, by an imaginative combination of authorial comment, well-conceived dramatic interactions, and the creation of icons from descriptions of furnishings, environments, and people's reading matter. Thus the reader experiences Webster through his domain, Tom his shed, Hector his restaurant, and Griselda her library.

The second chapter advances the plot and also provides the background concerning Hector and his struggles with his parents. Like Paul Dempster in *Fifth Business*, he is the son of a gloomy parson, who, in turn, is imprisoned by his own wan physique and possibly organic propensity to melancholy. Davies is good at presenting joyless states of mind, and he renders very credible the figure of John Mackilwraith, a man of "no deep devotion, no consciousness of hidden sources of strength, not even a rigid puritanism" (p. 74). He is a man devoid of dogma, joy, energy. The young Hector is expected to be a credit to his father and is associated with him by—and this is a neat stroke—

having to wear his cut-down clothing, including the clerical trousers transformed to knickerbockers, so that he is singled out "not only by his solemnity of expression, but by the startling blackness and shininess of his lower parts" (p. 74). The image suggests not only a Kafkaesque dung beetle but also the inheritance, at least as far as his sexual being is concerned, of his father's underdeveloped libido. There is an equally good description of Hector's mother, steeped in failure, whose world view consists only of expectations of catastrophe and whose miserable life is only mildly redeemed by her overprotective love for her son. She feeds him grossly and purges him with diabolical syrups, cathartics, and laxatives until his bowels have learned to behave "whimsically," a disability that affects his sex life in a most disastrous, though comical, fashion in later life. His adult fear of women and his inability to relate to them except in terms of *amour courtois* are thus linked directly to his controlling, overprotective mother. Pampered and overnurtured as he is, he can nevertheless rebel, and his treatment of a bully, named "Rat-face," at school is the first instance of his movement towards liberation, though his anger is sparked by a taunt directed at his mother. He beats Rat-face to a pulp and is extricated from him while the victim is "restored to such limited consciousness as his heredity and his fate permitted him to enjoy" (p. 79) — a remark that, in itself, hints at themes Davies will develop in later novels.

Hector fights again, this time with only superficial success, against his mother and the Presbyterian minister who succeeds his father. He protects his own vision of his future as a schoolteacher and deals with the pressure applied to him with spirit and firmness. Thus Chapter ii is mainly about Hector — his determination, planning, assiduity, common sense, and starved emotional self. It depicts his struggles in breaking away from the joylessness of his father and his mother's unimaginative ambitions. Her effect on him, however, is more permanent than he thinks, and it ruins his attempts to command Griselda's love.

"Pearl Vambrace," Davies says,

> lived a life which, to the casual glance, seemed unendurable. But she had grown up to it, and although she knew that it was not like the life of any other girl of her acquain-

tance she did not find it actively unpleasant. If the chance
had been offered to her, she would not have changed her lot
for that of anyone else; she would have asked, instead, that
a few changes be made in the life she had. (pp. 120–21)

She is imprisoned by the conflict between her parents — and, in
particular, that aspect of it which involves her mother's Catholic
mysticism, and consequent withdrawal, and her father's "chilly,"
self-approving stoicism — by the strict and confining morality of
the household, and the continuous demands the professor makes
in his attempts to turn her into a well-educated, docile, nicely
mannered wife he wished he'd had himself. Like Solly, like
Hector, she looks unconsciously and consciously for the magic of
The Tempest, the mysterious otherworldliness of the theatre, to
transform her life and free her. It is love, in Davies' romantic
view, that begins to stir the awareness in all these characters
that they live in physical and emotional situations from which
they need release, and specifically love, in Pearl's case, for the
attractive, dashing military man, Roger Tasset, who is to play
Ferdinand to her Miranda.

The Gonzalo role puts Hector in touch with the world of
romance; it is triggered by Griselda's kind words to him as she
drives Solly home. Later in the evening, he sees a pair of young
lovers embracing, thinks of Griselda as a possible mate, sleeps,
and is visited in the night by a dream of her, lightly clad, leaning
towards him with tenderness and speaking his name. Clearly this
is an anima figure, whom he, in his inexperience, misinterprets,
and so he falls in love with Griselda. The latter is already
perceived by Solly as a *belle dame sans merci*, and by Roger as a
potential name to be added to his list of seduced women. But
Hector's process is to withdraw from her in approved, classical
style and undergo the symptoms of loss of appetite and restless-
ness so well described by Ovid and Andreas Capellanus. He
makes the potentially liberating discovery that not every object
of a man's desire succumbs to planning and common sense.

Hector's love affair is in part pathetic, in part comic. Davies
does not seem quite certain how he feels about this central
character. The energy and sympathy expended upon Hector's
struggle to attain a foothold on life and to achieve independence
from his ghastly family seem, once he becomes a lover, to be

negated. It is true that there is always a preconsummatory clown-ishness about male lovers, as Chaucer shows in the *Troilus*, but I think Davies moves from such a satirical perspective on Hector to a dismissal. Hector's reliving the borborygmic embarrassment of his youth is certainly clownish, if overcontrived, but his clumsy attempt at suicide surely communicates a distress which ought to be taken more seriously by his creator. Instead, he is dismissed and nullified by the sententious discussion, very nearly a *literal* postmortem, between Humphrey Cobbler, the church organist and a sort of trickster figure in the trilogy, and Tom and Fredegonde, who close the novel just as they opened it:

> "Well, why did he do it?" said Cobbler.
>
> "Cheap religion," said Freddy.
>
> "The way we see it, sir," said Tom, after taking a second long draught of the champagne cider, "is like this. Too many people today are like this fellow Mackilwraith. They don't believe, and they haven't got the strength of mind to disbelieve. They won't get rid of religion, and they won't go after a religion that means anything. They just mess with religion. Now if this fellow Mackilwraith had been a believer — and I don't mind saying that I'm thinking of the C. of E. — he would have known that suicide is a sin, and his belief would have held him up in his trouble. And if he'd been an unbeliever he'd either have had too much guts to do it, or guts enough to finish it off proper. See?"
>
> "If he'd been a strong believer or a strong unbeliever he wouldn't have been pushed off his trolley just because he couldn't get to first base with Gristle," said Freddy. "Do you know, Tom, this isn't bad at all; just as soon as the apples come in, I'm going to get busy on a bigger and better batch."
>
> "Not bad," said Cobbler, "but not champagne. Just good cider with ideas above its station."
>
> "I know," said Freddy, a little sadly, "but you can't make something wonderful unless you start with the right stuff."
>
> "Like making a romantic lover out of Hector Mackil-wraith," said Solly. (pp. 281–82)

If this passage is meant to be revelatory of character, then the sympathy the novel has built up for each of the participants is dissipated. They are either stupid, or insensitive, or more likely both. Yet each has been defined as possessing a certain wisdom: Tom's is a gardener's wisdom, Freddy's a thoughtful and perceptive child / woman's, Solly's an academic's, and Cobbler's a literate and imaginative artist / roisterer's. It is most unlikely that Davies intends to undermine such people at the last minute by giving them cheap, callous, callow, wisecracking balderdash to utter. There is, for once, no authorial comment and no disjunction in tone between the narratorial voice and that of the characters, so it seems reasonable to suppose that judgements like "good cider with ideas above its station" are intended seriously by the author. Moreover, it is characteristic of Davies' subsequent work that he wishes to take religion seriously, to approach life from a "religious" perspective, to try to account for human experience using a "religious," and sometimes specifically Christian, vocabulary of ideas like "good," "evil," "spirit," "Devil," "God," and "Saint," and, above all, to employ a theme for his writing absolutely central to Christianity — that of "liberation."

This is not the place to embark on a discussion of "Liberation Theology," but it is worthwhile examining one paradigmatic passage of the New Testament to understand the religious basis of the notion of freedom and to consider how Davies has modified or diluted it. The passage is Acts xii. 5–11 and concerns the arrest of Peter by King Herod:

> Peter therefore was kept in prison; but prayer was made without ceasing of the church unto God for him.
> And when Herod would have brought him forth, the same night Peter was sleeping between two soldiers, bound with two chains; and the keepers before the door kept the prison.
> And, behold, the angel of the Lord came upon him, and a light shined in the prison; and he smote Peter on the side, and raised him up, saying, Arise up quickly. And his chains fell off from his hands.
> And the angel said unto him, Gird thyself, and bind on thy sandals. And so he did. And he saith unto him, Cast thy garment about thee, and follow me.
> And he went out, and followed him; and wist not that it

was true which was done by the angel; but thought he saw a vision.

When they were past the first and the second ward, they came unto the iron gate that leadeth unto the city; which opened to them of his own accord; and they went out, and passed on through one street; and forthwith the angel departed from him.

And when Peter was come to himself, he said, Now I know of a surety, that the Lord hath sent his angel, and hath delivered me out of the hand of Herod.....

Read metaphorically, this means, among other things, that Peter awakens to the fact that he *need not be a prisoner*, that he must follow his inner director, his private vision, and trust it, that when he succeeds in this the chains fall from him, for his imprisonment is only apparent, that even the solid iron gate, hitherto so invincible, opens of its own accord. Moreover, the event he thinks is illusory proves more real than the guards, the chains, the paraphernalia of bondage. And, when he "comes to himself," Peter realizes that this impulse towards freedom is a divine gift and divinely encouraged in him.

In *Tempest-Tost*, as I have noted, each of Solly, Pearl, and Hector possesses a vision, if only a very rudimentary one, of what it might be like to be "free"; each vision is based on the reaching out towards another human being. Though Hector fails to achieve Griselda and consequently drops back from the climax of his suicide attempt to his mundane, unvisionary self of common sense and pros and cons, there is nothing in the religion Davies refers to with such apparent approval to suggest that he or anybody else (whether in fiction or "real life") lacks the "right stuff" (whatever such an élitist phrase may mean) — like Rat-face, whose consciousness is so constrained by heredity and destinal forces — to actualize some future vision. Indeed, Hector's record in the achievement of visions is somewhat better than most of the other characters in the book. Davies seems here, and in his subsequent fiction, to adhere to the Laodiceanism levelled by Tom at Hector: as though he cannot make up his mind between the voluntarism that Christianity offers and the determinism at the back of his fascination with coincidence, synchronicity, fate, chance, and heredity. It is a hesitation which reduces the impact of his later works and which undermines his most interesting, though not necessarily his best, novel, *Fifth Business*.

The second Salterton novel is as engaging and amusing as *Tempest-Tost* and displays very similar faults and virtues. There is the same bland humour that Davies directs at Canadian attitudes towards life (the essays on editorials and on domestic architecture are examples),[48] and the same amused narratorial stance towards his characters and situations. A sly, mild wit illuminates some aspects of modern pedagogical attitudes, such as in the passage concerning Mr. Kelso and "Music Appreciation":

[Pearl] could appreciate anything, and satisfy Mr. Kelso that her appreciation was akin to, though naturally of a lesser intensity than, his own. Play her a Gregorian chant, and she would appreciate it; play her a Bartok quartet and she would appreciate that. (pp. 92–93)

Slightly less mild is the presentation of Norman and Dutchy, the reductive psychologist and his wife, which obviously reflects the 1950s concern with conformity that also found expression in such contemporary works as *The Lonely Crowd*, *White Collar*, and *The Organization Man*. The narrator of this novel is not developed much from that of the previous work; if anything, the essays are slightly longer, slightly more intrusive, than in *Tempest-Tost*.

Leaven begins with the figure of Gloster Ridley, depicted as a good man in search of an honorary degree from the local university as a final achievement of his career. He is considered slightly eccentric by his fellow townsfolk, and it is not until the end of the book that we are given to understand something about him. His desire for the outward trappings of success that a degree *honoris causa* would give him is evidently, and according to his own testimony, the result of a feeling that he is responsible for his wife's mental deterioration and her incarceration in a mental institution. But his eccentricities are not, despite Davies' efforts, made remarkable enough. The denouement, in the form of Ridley's confession to Mrs. Fielding, makes him too conscious of the reasons why the awarding of the degree would alleviate his guilt.

Ridley's involvements with his own guilt and various minor characters such as Shillito and Bevill Higgin are less important in the book than is the action involving Professor Vambrace. It is here that the novel's interest resides. Just as Hector's *furor* is central to *Tempest-Tost*, so is Vambrace's to *Leaven*. Furthermore, the character is better developed than any in the previous novel, and Davies does his best here to flesh out his creation with a psychological background which would make Vambrace's rage credible. We are told (Part III, passim) that he had, within an hour, worked himself up into a ferocious anger, which instead of expressing itself as outrage on behalf of his family, particularly Pearl whom the false marriage notice naturally concerns, seems directed outward from himself as though the hoax were a plot to discompose him personally. Pearl's mother cannot deal with this tremendous surge of rage and withdraws into weeping and praying, while Vambrace paces and glares with "unmistakable foam" (p. 95) at the corners of his lips, dredging from his stockpile of resentments his disappointment at not being elected Dean. "They" were mocking him and plotting against him, and now they wanted to disgrace him. He has rejected, according to the narrator, Pearl's mother's religion and forbidden Pearl to be brought up in the Catholic faith. In its place, he seems to have substituted a quasi-religious image of himself as the inheritor of the traits of the "Well-Born Celt,... cousin of the Marquis of Mourne and Derry" (p. 96); he therefore sees himself as proud and aristocratic, on the one hand, but full of wild, extravagant impulses, on the other. And, growing more and more caught up in this pleasing self-image, he even adopts a sort of brogue "punctuated by angry snorts and hollow laughter," a "mode of expression [which] owed a good deal to the plays of Dion Boucicault, which the Professor had seen in his boyhood" (p. 96). Yet his diatribe reveals the pathetic gap between his concept of himself as a Promethean rebel fighting a heroic battle against stupidity, Bumbledom, malice, and petty mindedness and the actions which his narrow life actually allows him: writing letters to the papers about garbage disposal and vaccination; and being outspoken at faculty meetings. He is a man whose sense of drama is perpetually frustrated by the trivia of everyday life. It is a malicious portrait, on the whole, but

Davies does not entirely alienate the reader's sympathy from what Vambrace calls "the aristocratic tradition, which is chiefly a tradition of not allowing oneself to be trampled over by a pack of louts and cheapjacks" (p. 103). His other delusions are depicted as more often pathetic than vicious, though their effect on Pearl, the only sympathetic member of the Vambrace family, is of course profound. Even here, though, Davies suggests, through a widening of the implications of the book's title, that good can arise from the negative components of human life, and that Vambrace's rage, domination, and cruelty provide a testing ground for Pearl, from which she arises triumphantly.

Thus, at the beginning of Part III, Pearl contemplates the relationship between her parents and sees clearly enough that Vambrace is a domestic tyrant and her mother his will-less victim. But because, as the narrator tells us, "...Pearl was a loyal daughter and it never occurred to her that home was, in many ways, a hell" (p. 95), she performs a mental trick of discounting her father's emotional effect on her by trivializing him to a "dozen-donut problem" (p. 94). She is not aware, in other words, of her own imprisonment and thus of the need to escape. Her first glimmerings that she is a prisoner and must begin evasive action have to do with a vague idea that it would be good to be married. She recognizes this impulse (p. 107) as one her parents would be hostile to and would attempt to repress. Thus her resistance to Vambrace's rage and to his threatening a lawsuit against Ridley and *The Bellman* is token only and subsidiary to the main issue, which is to accept the invitation to Yarrow's party. There is a struggle between Pearl and Vambrace over this invitation, which Pearl wins (she goes out); but so does Vambrace (he makes her guilty and ashamed). It is a well-presented interchange (p. 109), and symptomatic of a relationship that is parallel, as we discover later in the novel, to Solly's life with Mrs. Bridgetower. But Pearl's moment of awareness occurs during the finale of the party and is imposed, as seems perfectly natural, from the outside. It is sparked by Vambrace's fury, which, at the moment Solly is driving Pearl home, has reached its climax. The professor has dressed himself up, rather unbelievably, as a detective and has spent a fruitless evening following Gloster Ridley through the streets of Salterton. He has been detected and humiliated by Humphrey Cobbler, and is therefore already struggling with feelings of self-contempt. At the sight of his daughter with the son of an old faculty enemy, he explodes. He drags her from the car and cuffs her ear. Later,

> Pearl was still weeping, but silently, when dawn came through her window. She felt herself to be utterly alone and forsaken, for she knew that she had lost her father, more certainly than if he had died that night. (p. 141)

The blow on her ear, in other words, "saves" her and enables her to break free. And this freedom enables her to confess to Solly the facts about her homelife and how she had been cast into the "bitter role of the unmarried daughter who nurses both parents into the grave" (p. 213). A measure of her growing freedom is the fact that she can talk about this "without self pity" and with forgiveness of her parents:

> They have done everything they have done out of love. They loved each other very much, and I think they still do. . . . And they loved me as much as they were able. They did the best for me that they could — the best they knew. . . . But in spite of it all I love them very much. (p. 213)

This conclusion seems to accord nicely with Davies' sense, which emerges more clearly in the later novels, of the psychological importance of reconciliation and forgiveness between child and parents—that for one's own wholeness it is not only necessary to break from one's parents, but also to be reconciled with them, even, perhaps, united with them in a new way.

Solly is imprisoned by his useless passion for Griselda Webster, a theme announced in *Tempest-Tost*, by his need to produce as an academic and his consequent involvement in the unedifying works of Charles Heavysege, and, above all, by his mother. That the latter is formidable is hinted at in the earlier novel; in *Leaven of Malice*, Davies casts her in a slightly different light. He shows us how Mrs. Bridgetower, during one of her "at homes," is able to demolish, in a quite masterly fashion, the elderly ladies comprising her tea-drinking circle. She maintains a physical posture of domination but slumps exhaustedly when the company leaves, and Solly has to take her upstairs to her bedroom and administer her medicines. During the debate that follows, however, concerning Vambrace's libel suit, anger makes the old lady drop twenty years. Though Solly's growing reluctance to be cross-examined by her on the subject of Pearl causes her some anxiety, "...she was so stimulated by hatred and the love of combat that she was able to retain some composure, and contented herself by saying that she hoped that in the morning he would be in a more reasonable frame of mind, and see things as she saw them" (p. 158).

He is able, however, to be evasive with her about his feelings, despite the subtlety of her questions and the obvious, manipulative style in which she asks them. "What a demon she was!" he thinks (p. 215), yet he begins to pity her and this pity makes him think even more strongly of Pearl, as though Pearl were an instrument from the outside to make him finally aware of the urgency of the choice before him:

> How easy, how utterly simple, for Solly to turn back to Mother—to drive away the powerful but still strange vision of Veronica, and to give herself to Mother forever!... Thus life and death warred in Solly's bosom in the night, and in her bedroom his mother lay, yearning for him, willing him to come to her. (p. 216)

Mrs. Bridgetower is seen in this novel in all her vulnerability and pathos. It does not make her a sympathetic figure, but nor does it make her evil. In fact, there seems little room for evil in Davies' cosmos. Even the perpetrator of the hoax, Bevill Higgin, is more a Jungian trickster figure — an imp of malice, whose activities, though they cause pain, also change in minute ways the society in which they have their context. This is ably put by the Dean of the Cathedral in his "leaven of malice" speech (pp. 215–52). But in may respects Mrs. Bridgetower is the archetypal Terrible Mother, devouring and insatiable, from whom, as Solly perceives, he must break free or lose his life.

A Mixture of Frailties is part of the trilogy only to the extent that its action begins and ends in Salterton, that some characters from the earlier works appear in it, and that certain small-town attitudes are examined and criticized. Its heroine does not appear in

the other two novels, and its locale is European, chiefly London.
One, at any rate, of the Salterton themes is developed — the
combination of pathos and manipulation observed in Mrs.
Bridgetower becomes, by her death, almost pure malevolence.
Solly's marriage to Pearl — rechristened Veronica in this book —
has devastated her and is possibly a contributory factor in her
death. Her will, by which the young couple inherits her considerable fortune only if they succeed in producing a male heir, is her
revenge on them. On the other hand, the will benefits Monica
Gall since the income from the fortune must go to the support
and training in the arts of some talented girl, so that it is possible
to consider even Mrs. Bridgetower's malice as a form of leaven.
Humphrey Cobbler's epitaph to her — *"Toujours gai, le diable est
mort"*[49] — seems to encapsulate prevailing Salterton opinion
most precisely, and also Davies' own. Despite this, Solly is still
troubled by her and still finds himself defending her. He has
fought bravely for his freedom and, by marrying Veronica, won;
yet the old woman's "dead hand" continues to raise issues even
more profound than the question of a cruel will.

On the whole, though, Davies' interest in this book seems to
have transferred itself to the struggles of Monica to become a
professional singer. The novel is therefore more of an ordinary
Bildungsroman, and, though not without interest, it lacks the
edge of its more belletristic predecessors. Davies has "developed"
as a novelist from the slapdash techniques of the earlier books
towards a more conventional pursuit of "character" and "plot."
He has thus sacrificed much of the satiric thrust, though the main
characters, Monica herself and the novel's more demonic figures
such as Giles Revelstoke and Murtagh Molloy, come across more
credibly to the reader. These, and the pompous figure of Sir
Benedict Domdaniel, take over from the narrator of the earlier
fiction the job of delivering sententious pronouncements on art
and life, ranging from a simplified exposition of the Freudian
categories of Eros and Thanatos with regard to classification of
human beings by types, to Molloy's definitions of "mood." The
total effect is not always very successful: on the one hand, the
figures emerge more clearly as Davies' interest in building a credible narrative grows; on the other, the comparative subordina-
tion of the narrator to a minor role results in his male characters
having to bear a double load — as essential players in a plot and

as essayists on a variety of topics. Moreover, Davies tries to over-come the detached puppetry to which the omniscient narrative mode can degenerate by moving uneasily between a diminished omniscience and an attempt to observe the novel's action through Monica's consciousness — which he fails to render very convincingly.

The theme of liberation from family and background is part of *Mixture*'s structure, but much less so than before, and is announced by Domdaniel, who sees it as a necessary part of Monica's professional development that she overcome a "stultifying home atmosphere and cultural malnutrition" (p. 54). This, of course, was precisely Hector Mackilwraith's problem as it is to be, in a much more complex way, Dunstan Ramsay's in *Fifth Business*, and Davies' solution for his heroine is a systematic emotional and cultural education. Monica seems to make the break with the negative part of her upbringing without much communicated sense of struggle, as though Davies had worked this theme through and was finished with it. Such, of course, is not the case as the Deptford trilogy shows. What Davies attempts in *Mixture* is to move beyond family and small-town circum-stances to considering the effects on Monica's growth of a series of mentors: her mother, Molloy, Giles, and finally Domdaniel are all absorbed by her in turn and used as a means of judging and discarding previous patterns as she sees the world and human experience through their eyes. And as she moves forward, each, with the exception of Domdaniel, the last, dies a real or symbolic death: her mother, with cancer; Molloy, by making a drunken pass at her (she "cracks" Molloy "smartly over the skull" with a "formidable bludgeon" [p. 259]); and Giles, by staging a suicide which turns, by misadventure, into the real thing. For each of these events, Monica bears some responsibility, as though Davies intends to present the idea that she brings about her own devel-opment through a progressive rejection of these same mentors.

Nevertheless, Monica Gall's liberation is not very strongly presented as a psychological struggle, and, as *Bildungsroman*, the book is undermined by its central character's ordinariness. She is basically a sensible, stable, rather hefty, normal girl, who appears more bovine than temperamental. But for the accident of a powerful singing voice, it is not clear why she would not have chosen to remain in Salterton, or some place like it, as a typist or file clerk, pursuing first marriage as an alternative career, then childraising. It is true that in retrospect, and considered in the totality of Davies' works to date, it could be argued, as F. L. Radford argues,[50] that certain Jungian concepts of the structure of human personality underlie *A Mixture of Frailties,* as though Davies had read his Jung thoroughly before setting up his characters so carefully as one another's animas and animuses. Radford claims that the mother archetype, for instance, pervades this novel, as it does *Fifth Business*, and in a fairly complex way: Mrs. Bridgetower is a "possessive demon" to Solly and a "good fairy" to Monica, though this seems less Jungian than it does Daviesian — an irony based on his essentially comic vision that life is complex and many-sided. Yet there seems more truth in the idea that Monica is an anima figure to Giles and he, though more of a petulant, spoiled brat with a psychotic undertone to his personality than a "satanic genius," is an animus figure.

Radford quotes Davies as saying in *Mixture* (in his narrator's persona) that *The Golden Asse*, on which Giles's opera is based, is an allegory "disclosing the metamorphosis of life itself, in which man moves from confident inexperience through the bitterness of experience, toward the rueful wisdom of self-knowledge" (p. 316). This seems to be what it is Davies' intention to depict in the Deptford trilogy. Here it is presented rather weakly, for if there is much in Monica's life that is inherently bitter — her mother's death, Giles's behaviour towards her, culminating in his suicide — each circumstance is fortuitous and presented as such. Thus *A Mixture of Frailties* is indeed a transitional novel, as writers on Davies claim it is, but it is less interesting than its two predecessors and more conventional than either they or its successors.

It is generally claimed that, so far in his career, *Fifth Business* is Davies' richest and most accomplished novel. It was published at the end of a twelve-year novelistic silence and is markedly different in intention, if not in tone, from the earlier work. It is clear from Davies' own account that it was conceived somewhat earlier than 1960, about the time *Mixture* appeared, for his notes for a new work at that time suggest the locale of *Fifth Business*, Deptford, and one of its themes — that of revenge — which, he claims, he amended in the direction of a study of guilt.[51] Davies observes that Canadian reviewers did not, generally speaking, like the novel when it appeared in 1970. They expected him to maintain his stance as a *comic* novelist and did not care for the new "seriousness" he manifested in *Fifth Business*. American critics, however, praised the book enthusiastically, and Davies responded by writing another novel as a follow-up in the same vein: *The Manticore*.

In *Fifth Business*, the opening episode deals with the unlucky flight of the snowball thrown by Percy Boyd Staunton, which changes the lives of the Dempster family and also sets the course for the life of Dunstan Ramsay, the book's hero, who feels he must expiate his sense of guilt for his part in the disaster. Percy, however, feels no guilt, and Davies' problem is to tell the story of Percy, extrovert and egotist, while at the same time feeling a lack of sympathy for such a point of view. In *The Manticore*, then, Davies tells the story from the son's, David Staunton's, perspective,

> who was compelled, as children often are, to live out the unlived portion of his father's life. (Davies, "The Deptford Trilogy in Retrospect," p. 9)

The warm response to these books, Davies claims, compelled him to give his public more of what it seemed to be asking for with *World of Wonders*, told from Paul Dempster's viewpoint through the agency of Dunstan Ramsay.

This trilogy, as it turned out to be, has created for Davies an international reputation and probably one of the widest audiences ever for a Canadian writer. There has been some critical commentary on the books, the best of it collected in *Studies in Robertson Davies' Deptford Trilogy*, in which meanings, surprising to Davies himself, have been discovered. He comments that such meanings are quite possibly valid since a book of any value must be a story, must provide some substance for allegory, and must say something about the human condition to which the reader can give serious attention:

> The story of the trilogy is plain enough: a happening which is only in part an accident sets in motion a train of incidents

that strongly influence the lives of three men, and each man's personality determines the way in which he accepts what comes to him. To one it brings revelation; to another disillusionment and death; to the third wealth, fame and revenge. (Davies, "The Deptford Trilogy in Retrospect," pp. 10–11)

Davies refuses to comment on the allegorical component of the trilogy for the excellent reason that it is not his job — a writer, he claims, is in a dangerous frame of mind when he thinks of himself as an allegorist (unless he sets out to write an allegory), and it is up to others to disentangle what allegorical threads there are. The third element, the comment on the human condition, is bound up with Davies' concept of the importance of coincidence in life, of the operation of destiny, and of those forces residing in a man's unconscious that shape his existence.

Though *Fifth Business* opens with the snowball scene, its main narrative device is set out in the second section as a report that the narrator, Dunstan Ramsay, makes to the headmaster of his private school protesting an accolade appearing in the school newspaper on the occasion of his retirement. This accolade dismisses him, though affectionately, as a harmless old buffer who knows little outside the school he has taught at for forty-five years. It turns out, however, that Ramsay is not only a recipient of the Victoria Cross, but also the author of ten books reaching wide audiences, a contributor to the *Analecta Bollandiana*, etc., who has come to the full stature of a man with a rich, complex, and gratifying life outside the school. Furthermore, fate has carved for him the "vital though never glorious role of Fifth Business"[52] in the major personal relationships in his career — with Mrs. Dempster and Percy Boyd Staunton.

Thus it is that Ramsay introduces himself. Behind the apparently bland and dull exterior there lies this fascinating, intelligent, courageous, intense, and active man, whose life both externally and interiorly is as rich as anybody's. The relationship between the headmaster and Ramsay is not pursued, however; it is merely a device to provide a context, or rationale, for Davies' first-person monologue.

As in the earlier novels, the first major conflict of which the hero becomes aware is the one involving his mother. She is a rigid, domineering woman of some generous impulses, as her treatment of the "simple" Mrs. Dempster indicates, and of a Scottish Presbyterian rigidity and narrowness of moral vision. Her house is clean to the point of sterility, from which Dunstan retreats to the village library imbibing books on magic and conjuring, busy about acquiring powers to enable him to deal with the world. This sets up the incident of the stolen egg, with which Dunstan practises and whose theft he denies. This scene, with Mrs. Ramsay working herself up into an almost insane frenzy of righteous anger and revenge (the whip) and the consequent atonement, with the young Dunstan forced to beg her forgiveness, then God's, on bended knees, is quite brilliantly handled and understated. On the one hand, the young Dunstan, unready as yet to fully question his mother's values, believes he is unworthy of God's clemency and tends to perceive his borrowing of the egg through her eyes. On the other hand, he is puzzled by the discrepancy between a general concept of "motherliness" and his mother's actual behaviour. The reader, however, is invited to view this episode with more detachment, so that Dunstan's response to his mother is seen as pert and humorous, her immediate reaction, insane and sadistic, and her subsequent manipulations of him ("I know I'll never have another anxious moment with my own dear laddie" [p. 35]), disgusting.

The contrast Davies sets up is between this factual and rigid woman and the mysterious Mrs. Dempster, who has been wounded and "simplified" by the snowball and the consequent premature birth of her son Paul, and yet who is granted healing powers. Dunstan befriends Mrs. Dempster to the point where Mrs. Ramsay forces him to choose between "her" and "that woman" (p. 69). World War I having conveniently broken out, Dunstan solves the problem, and temporarily evades the choice, by enlisting in the army. It is here that the concept of liberation, so much the theme of the earlier trilogy, is modified and made more subtle. In the Deptford books, it is transmuted into a Jungian idea of individuation: the struggle is not only to rid oneself of one's parents in some sort of physical sense, but to discover what they are to one's psychic life, to come to grips with their residues in that psyche, and to somehow surmount them or at least become familiar with them. The central conflict, as F. L. Radford points out in a very useful article,[53] is between two aspects of the maternal in a man's life: the Pieta and the Terrible. In the first, the mother is perceived as smiling, loving, life-affirming, and life-giving; in the second, as demonic, devouring, and castrating. Dunstan Ramsay's own mother is both aspects, though the Terrible predominates.

As the source of his guilts and hesitations in later life, it is she who produces in him a hard, acerbic exterior. She appears in his life later as an aspect of Diana, the girl who nurses him back to health after his wounding in the war and who initiates him into sexual life, for Ramsay sees Diana as devouring, as a woman who wishes to possess him and to make him over to something she wants him to be. Much of Ramsay's life is the attempt to realize consciously the unconscious sources of his own personality. He projects the Terrible Mother image once more onto Liesl, Eisengrim's assistant, who, in a comic scene, gives him the greatest sexual pleasure he has ever experienced after first wrestling with him, then beating him over the head with his own artificial limb, a symbol of her masculine component prefigured, in Ramsay's personal mythology, by the "bearded lady" image which so engrosses him.

The anima in its more positive manifestation, the Pieta, Ramsay projects onto Mrs. Dempster, whose madness, if that is what it is, he has helped to create from his own role in the snowball incident. She is a saint figure, a Virgin Mary, a woman clothed with the sun from the book of Revelation, a "fool-saint," and, in her role as the woman who gave herself to the tramp in the pit because "...he wanted it so badly" (p. 49), a kind of trickster or, as Radford calls her, taboo-breaker. Later on she is an old woman, quite simply, on the point of death, her magical dimensions almost gone. Yet when she dies, her function in his life is revealed to him in a dream of her opposite:

> It was a very bad night for me. I kept up a kind of dismal stoicism until I went to bed, and then I wept. I had not done such a thing since my mother had beaten me so many years before.... When at last I fell asleep I dreamed frightening dreams, in some of which my mother figured in terrible forms. (p. 287)

The mother function, in other words, is perceived here as being dual — the Pieta aspect cannot be experienced without the negative, Terrible side, the reverse of the coin. Shortly after this, he encounters the Pieta of his dreams, the "Little Madonna," in the cathedral at Salzburg.

Ramsay can only liberate himself from this fear of the Terrible Mother by confronting it in its fullest, most demonic manifestation — Liesl. Liesl, along with Leola, Mrs. Dempster, Faustina, Boy Staunton's second wife, Denyse, and Diana, are all aspects of Ramsay's anima projected onto "real-life" women, and it is through interaction and confrontation with them, and finally physical battle culminating in a friendship, that he grows towards psychic health.

Thematically, then, *Fifth Business* both fulfils and amplifies the liberation motif of the Salterton trilogy. It is certainly a more ambitious novel than any which preceded it, though, formally speaking, it resembles them fairly closely. In this respect, it may be of interest to apply the term "satiric romance"[54] to the novel as a description of its form. There are, for instance, strong satiric elements in the early sections as Ramsay examines and criticizes his rural childhood background — the values of his parents and of the community beyond, their Calvinism, self-righteousness, malice, pomposity, life-denial, *kakoethia*, and general hick-town ignorance, expressed most precisely in a good imitation of Ring Lardner's "Haircut" (pp. 117–21). In places, the satire extends further, as in this passage describing the victory celebrations at Deptford and the hanging of the Kaiser in effigy:

> ...some of them were much too small to know what hanging was, or what a Kaiser might be, but I cannot call them innocent, for they were being as vicious as their age and experience allowed. And the people in the crowd, as I looked at them, were hardly recognizable as the earnest citizens who, not half an hour ago, had been so biddable under the spell of patriotic oratory, so responsive to *Canadian Born*, so touched by the romantic triangle of Leola, and Percy, and myself. Here they were, in this murky, fiery light, happily acquiescent in a symbolic act of cruelty and hatred. As the only person there, I suppose, who had any idea of what a really bad burn was like, I watched them with dismay that mounted towards horror, for these were my own people. (p. 115)

There is something here of the antiwar satires of such writers as Aldington, Graves, and Sassoon, who are even more disturbed by the depravity and blood-lust of their fellow citizens than by the horrors of the trenches, for their basic attitude is a combatant's contempt for the bellicosity of the skrimshanker and the beer-parlour general. It should be noted, however, that Davies is more accepting of his countrymen's failings and more detached about them. The satiric attacks are generally carried off with great energy, but with a lack of real hate, so that Ramsay comes across as an open-eyed, but basically loving and forgiving, human being. This sympathetic characterization serves Davies well, for it enables him to render with some authority Ramsay's later and far more dubious propositions.

The novel more importantly establishes a satiric contrast between two ways of being in the world: Boy Staunton's, which is basically a Mammon-serving rationality connoting success, power, ambition, empiricism, money, and sexual conquest; and Ramsay's, connoting a sense of myth, rhythm, and pattern in human life, together with the principles of modesty, humility, asceticism, self-discipline, and chastity. It is true that there is much in Ramsay that denies life, and that his sexuality is starved, like Hector Mackilwraith's, through parent-induced guilt and timidity, but the movement of the novel is an account of his spiritual and psychological growth, of his liberation from the shackles with which his parents have bound him. Staunton's notion of growth (and, by extension, that of his middle- and upper-class compatriots) is confined to a consideration of his stock-market portfolio. The novel's satire, then, affirms Ramsay's values, tentative and embryonic at any given stage though they may be, and denies Staunton's, which are fixed, rigid, and sterile.

The romance aspect of *Fifth Business* has to do with its "quest" motif. Ramsay begins the quest by finding himself reading, to the young Paul Dempster, a book about saints, and he acquires a personal saint, Paul's mother, for whose "simplification" he feels some guilt. Later, lying badly wounded in a demolished Flemish church, he sees Mrs. Dempster's face on a statue of the Virgin and Child, and this is the epiphany which starts him on a journey of discovery, both personal and general, concerning saints, their lives, their links with the magical and the numinous, and the role they play, or seem to play, in human life. This fascination with hagiology leads Ramsay to the Bollandists, to Liesl, and to a reunion, after many years, with Paul Dempster. Thus the saint theme is the motor which propels the plot and lends it considerable interest and excitement. Unfortunately, it is also the source of the book's weaknesses. For one thing, the novel projects a sense of clutter and confusion: saints, magic, myth, and coincidence — there is so much Ramsay has to say about them, and so many connections among them he wishes to make. The many opinions expressed in the book — by the narrator, Liesl, Padre Blazon, and others — make of the novel's fabric a sort of filigree work spun out of people's heads, with very little feeling in it, except in the early chapters. And the opinions, as intellectual statements, seem feeble and reductive. "Everything in *Fifth Business*," a student once told me, "is like everything else." It would be well here to consider a typical passage which illustrates this flaw. In the last dialogue with Padre Blazon, Ramsay describes his battle with Liesl, and, at the point when the priest asks him if he had succeeded in meeting the Devil, he says,

> I met Him in Mexico City. He was disguised as a woman — an extremely ugly woman but unquestionably a woman.... The Devil proved to be a very good fellow. (p. 293)

As though to ignore the inanity of this, the priest replies,

> The Devil knows corners of us all of which Christ Himself is ignorant. Indeed, I am sure Christ learned a great deal that was salutary about Himself when He met the Devil in the wilderness. Of course, that was a meeting of brothers; people forget too readily that Satan is Christ's elder brother and has certain advantages in argument that pertain to a senior. (p. 293)

This, like many of Davies' pronouncements (and they remain Davies' when uttered by a fictional character of whom he approves), is worth examining as characteristic of Davies' later mode. First there is a quality of deliberate, and by no means unattractive, iconoclasm about it. The idea of Christ ignorant of certain "corners" of us, or of Satan as Christ's elder brother, strikes me as theological nonsense, though playful enough, and delivered with a certain breeziness. It is the kind of thing that Hilaire Belloc might have said to Wing-Commander Maurice Baring. And there is, I fancy, something of Belloc in Padre Blazon himself, with his response to the Dunstanesque tonging of the Devil's nose: "You met the Devil as an equal, not cringing or frightened or begging for a trashy favour. That is the heroic life..." (p. 294). Blazon goes on to tell Ramsay that he is "fit to be the Devil's friend, without any fear of losing [him]self to Him" (p. 294). Again, we can almost hear the crashing of Belloc's tankard on the oak table in the taproom of the Inn at the End of the World. There seems, however, to be an elementary confusion here between the negative forces in the human personality and Evil seen as some sort of external force personified by the Devil. The first needs a psychiatrist, the second, theologically speaking, God's intervention and protection. Padre Blazon, the reader might hope, would know the difference. Davies does not convince me that *he* knows it. Evil is surely, and within Davies' own religious frame, not to be trivialized or secularized as something that can be handled by a trip to Zurich and glibly spoken of as a Shadow in oneself with which one "comes to terms." While Davies' Jungian superstructure, with its concepts of synchronicity, coincidence, animas, and shadows, is interesting and used inventively, there is a fundamental lack of seriousness about it in Davies's hands, as though he himself only half-believed what he so energetically presents.

The Manticore is narrated in the first person by David Staunton, son of the Boy Staunton of *Fifth Business*, a successful trial lawyer known for his championing of the underdog, or at least of men and women who look like they might be underdogs. He is, as the book opens, voluntarily undergoing a Jungian psychoanalysis conducted by a Doctor von Haller. Like all sequels, this novel must solve the technical problem of using characters and unresolved situations from a preceding work while presenting itself autonomously as a viable fiction. Davies solves the problem by narrating the story from a different perspective, by dealing with a largely separate set of events, and by changing the format of the novel so that it consists of a verbatim account of interviews with the doctor, interspersed with autobiographical essays.

There is thus a considerable structural difference between this novel and the one that precedes it, a difference which Davies uses wisely to obscure the fact that David's "voice" is not dissimilar to Ramsay's, which, in turn, is not vastly different from that of the earlier trilogy's third-person narrator.

Most readers, I think, can assent readily enough to *The Manticore*'s interview format as a mode of narration. The narrative itself, however, is very often diluted by the blow-by-blow account of the analysis experience and, in particular, by the necessary but somewhat chalk-and-blackboard use of psychoanalytic jargon. Nevertheless, this does not become oppressive until the end of the novel. The narrative increases in interest and tension as David speaks of his experiences with alcohol and of his father's murder, with its aftermath of the burial and of conflict with Denyse (David's stepmother). There is a fine, Grand Guignol passage dealing with Denyse's attempt to acquire a death mask, for she employs a dentist friend to cover the corpse's face with a plastic that only the undertakers, using hammers and chisels, can remove. Possibly this is supposed to suggest Denyse's attempt to control her husband even in death by fixing him in a permanent likeness according to how she sees him. At the same time, the shiny coating of plastic over Boy's face is an image of the superficial nature of his life of correct, chic appearance.

At any rate, the major theme of the novel is clear and announced early. David must emerge from the shadow cast by his powerful father, who has tried to control him by withholding his love and approval, and who, even in death, by the old-fashioned device of a will (used, of course, in *A Mixture of Frailties*), has expressed his disappointment with David for his lack of wife and lack of apparent interest in women, and for his consequent failure to produce an heir. The father who emerges from these pages — snobbish, sexually attractive, immensely energetic and ambitious — is perhaps a little bloodless and something of a caricature, but he is rendered to us through David's perceptions and his *overwhelming* quality is believable enough. David must achieve release from this paternalism and a peaceful resolution of his conflict with Boy Staunton.

Davies pays considerable attention to a description of David's childhood, and here, particularly, there are echoes of previous novels. For instance, the protagonist is afflicted, as was Hector

Mackilwraith, by the imaginations of his bowel-obsessed elders, though the effects on David's life of the patent cures and laxatives with which he is tormented are not made obviously influential on the course of his adult life. Indeed, the business of "Doctor Tyrrell's Domestic Internal Bath" seems hardly integral to the plot (unless to provide a comic backdrop to von Haller's question concerning sodomy) and instead functions as a separable essay or, within the context of the fiction, as a sort of verbal *lazzo*. More importantly, one of the motifs of the novels recurs in *The Manticore*: Mrs. Bridgetower, the Terrible Mother, and her later manifestation as Mrs. Ramsay, appears as Denyse, while Leola is a sort of enfeebled Pieta. This childhood ends, however, when David's sister Caroline speculates one memorable evening that their mother was murdered and that David is Ramsay's son. As Doctor von Haller says:

> ...she put your beautiful mother in a different perspective, as somebody over whom men might quarrel, and whom another woman might think it worthwhile to murder.[55]

David's account makes vivid two other people essential to his development, or lack of it. The first is an Anglican priest named Father Knopwood, who prepares him for confirmation and who initiates him to the spiritual and moral worlds, and the other is his father's old mistress, Myrrha Martindale, who initiates him into the sexual. It is Boy who sets David up, who stage-manages the dinner party, and who exits at the appropriate moment. He therefore controls even David's sex life. David's emotions in adolescence are focused on the innocent Judy Wolff — this relationship is discouraged by the girl's father, who actually presents David with an ultimatum. Helplessly dominated by these two powerful adult male figures, he turns quite savagely against Father Knopwood, whose consolation he finds cold:

> Now you have had some skilful instruction in the swordsman-and-amorist game. What is it? Nothing but the cheerful trumpet-and-drum of the act of kind. Simple music for simple souls. Is that what you want with Judy? Because that is what her father fears. He doesn't want his daughter's life to be blighted by a whoremaster's son and, as he very shrewdly suspects, a whoremaster's pupil. (p. 184)

At the point in his analysis when he reports this dialogue to von Haller, he remarks that he cannot forgive Knopwood for trying to "blacken" his father. He rejects Knopwood's position that a man must choose his own moment for sexual initiation, and he also rejects von Haller's defence of this position. Yet, much later in his analysis, he is able to say:

> I had come to hate the fact that I had been initiated into the world of physical sex in something Father had stage-managed. It wasn't sex itself, but Father's proprietorial way with it, and with me.... I wanted no more of it. It seemed like following in the swordsman's footsteps.... (p. 228)

Knopwood's analysis of the relationship between David and Boy Staunton is excellently stated, and, within its context, convincing. It seems as though Davies is firmly on David's side— indeed, the latter's turnaround concerning his first sexual experience suggests this. Knopwood's affirmation of such traditional concepts as honour, sacrifice, and love is resented by David at the time, but is seen later as decisive:

> I still adored [my Father], but my adoration was flawed with doubts. That was why I determined not to try to be like him, not to permit myself any thought of rivalling him but to try to find some realm where I could show that I was worthy of him.
> DR. VON HALLER: My God, what a fanatic!
> MYSELF: That seems a rather unprofessional outburst.
> DR. VON HALLER: Not a bit. You are a fanatic. Don't you know what fanaticism is? It is overcompensation for doubt. (p. 191)

I quote this passage also to demonstrate the glibness of some of Davies' writing, which grows more and more shrill in the last two books. "Fanaticism is overcompensation for doubt." What genuine, sensitive psychiatrist would unload such a fortune-cookie motto on a patient of David Staunton's intelligence? Yet, increasingly, Davies writes as though he believed such adages himself. Despite lapses, however, the novel proceeds satisfactorily to a point where David's liberation, at least as regards his father, is almost complete. The process culminates in a dream wherein David sees his father ascending into the sky. His trousers drop and his naked buttocks are revealed. This dream is linked in the narrative to the way God reveals himself to Moses in Exodus but seems more to suggest that passage in Jung's *Memories, Dreams, Reflections* in which the author describes losing his terror of God and blissfully accepting the possibility of Grace:

> I saw before me the cathedral, the blue sky. God sits on His golden throne, high above the world — and from under the throne an enormous turd falls upon the sparkling new roof, shatters it, and breaks the walls of the cathedral asunder.[56]

Though this vision, like David's, is endowed with a certain risibility, it signifies an end to a stage in Jung's own growth. David's humanization of his father through the agency of the dream indicates an end to his awe regarding his father, and his exaggerated respect for law, system, reason, and authority — all of which he has internalized as his own judge: Mr. Justice Staunton.

Had Davies finished the novel here, he would have succeeded in creating a tense and vivid fiction "about" a man achieving a self-defining act of liberation with the help of a course of psychoanalysis, conveyed to the reader vividly and, for all I know, accurately. But the novel is enfeebled by its lengthy conclusion, in which David encounters, quite fortuitously, the grotesque and unlikely couple, Ramsay and Liesl, at Saint Gall, and the novel ends in an absurd, speleological meandering through the caverns above Sorgenfrei. This journey is difficult enough for the hero (and for the reader) to endure without the additional burdens of pseudo-symbolism (bear-worship) and the pseudo-profound remarks made by Liesl as a running, or perhaps crawling, commentary, as each stage of this "re-birth" is achieved:

> Awe is a very unfashionable, powerful feeling. (p. 267)

> [Rebirth] is learning to know oneself as fully human.... It's certainly not crawling back into your mother's womb; it's more a re-entry and return from the womb of mankind. A fuller comprehension of one's humanity. (pp. 267–68)

> Man is a noble animal, Davey. Not a good animal; a noble animal. (p. 273)

It seems that Davies insists on injecting into his carefully representationalist fable the elements of mystery and surprise to reinforce his basic message that these are inextricably interwoven with quotidian events. This is unexceptionable, yet the mumbojumbo into which the novel degenerates serves only to undermine that genuine sense of mystery of David's life, of any life, communicated so adequately and effortlessly in the preceding narrative.

World of Wonders completes the Deptford trilogy with an account of the life of Mrs. Dempster's prematurely born son, Paul. The events in this life are sensational enough: Paul is first a sort of white slave to an illusionist named Willard in a travelling carnival show, then an understudy and double for an actor-manager, Sir John Tresize, then a mender of clockwork toys (during which period he meets Liesl), and finally the master illusionist of international repute, Magnus Eisengrim, responsible, *inter alia*, for the elaborate Brazen Head routine, which so dramatically ends *Fifth Business*. The novel is therefore packed with material of considerable intrinsic interest — circuses, vaudeville, the stage, repertory companies on the move, nineteenth-century melodramas, mechanical gadgets such as Abdullah, the Card-Playing Automaton, based presumably on Maelzel's delightful chess-playing machine — some of it presented as *lazzi*, some in the form of explicatory essays, but not enough of it in the form of fully realized fiction. The novel, in fact, seems top-heavy with information, and its central character oddly, and not credibly, detached from his own very vivid experiences. Paul does not come across to the reader as much more than an information source, though the detail on its own is sufficiently entertaining to support the narrative.

Davies uses a frame device to present Paul's history. The prime narrator is Dunstan Ramsay, who controls the flow of Paul's information by cutting it off at critical and suspenseful moments to tell the reader the less interesting frame story, which deals with the interactions between Paul and a group of filmmakers, who have some to consult him about a TV script dealing with the magician Robert-Houdin. Ramsay uses the filmmakers as a means of commenting editorially on Paul's account and personality, and as a way of increasing the reader's sense of Paul as an exceedingly skilful and manipulative showman.

The shifts of perspective and narratorial stance inherent in Davies' method are very cleverly handled, and, technically, *World of Wonders* seems flawless to me. But the characterizations and, above all, the *subject matter* are lacking in sharp focus. It is not at all clear what the fiction is *about*. Solly Bridgetower, Pearl Vambrace, Hector Mackilwraith, Dunstan Ramsay, David Staunton, even Monica Gall, are all deeply engaged in a struggle for psychic freedom in their journey towards wholeness, so that the novels preceding *World of Wonders* communicate a genuine tension, despite their intermittent flaws of weak prose, prolixity, and editorialism. But Eisengrim's struggles are conducted on the more trivial level of external adventure; the early circus scenes involving Paul's imprisonment by the abominable Willard, though described with great energy and a much fuller grasp of the elements of style than exists in the earlier work, lack any sense of real struggle. There is no good reason why Paul should remain with this diabolical circus other than the fact that had he not done so there would be no entertaining description of carnival life. Similarly, the material concerning Sir John Tresize seems to exist in the novel for its own sake, as a means whereby Davies can communicate what he knows about Sir John Martin-Harvey and his troupe, which toured Canada in the 1920s.

Like *The Manticore*, *World of Wonders* degenerates into sophomoric discussions between various of the characters about Life, the Devil, Sin, Art, Illusion, Reality, and so on — discussions in which the sententious Liesl figures strongly. Yet it *does* provide a different perspective on the events of the two earlier novels. Eisengrim's view of his mother, for instance, is entirely different from Ramsay's, who regards her as a saint; and his attitude towards Boy Staunton, whose importance to himself, Ramsay, and David Staunton he does not understand until Boy's last day, is quite neutral. Again, however, the interest thus generated is insufficient to sustain *World of Wonders* as a work of fiction in its own right.

Robertson Davies' career as an editor, playwright, novelist, teacher, essayist, and literary critic is, by Canadian standards, an extraordinary one. He is not only judged successful by the conventional, middlebrow standards of the literate anglophones who constitute his chief audience, he *is* successful in that his achievements are commensurate with his considerable, multifaceted talents. He is, in other words, not only a best-selling, mid-cult novelist, but a serious artist. Yet the sheer variety and copiousness of his writing makes the task of assessment difficult, particularly when so much of it is occasional and journalistic. In my opinion, his best work is to be found in *Tempest-Tost*, *Leaven of Malice*, *Fifth Business*, and in the first three-quarters of *The Manticore*. The Marchbanks volumes, the other novels, and the reviews and critical essays all deserve an attention I have been unable to provide in this essay, but their interest, in comparison with the books I've mentioned, is minor.

Davies' faults are prolixity, compositional sloppiness, sententiousness, and, very often, intellectual and emotional shallowness. His great virtues are energy, wit, an essentially comic vision, *sprezzatura*, a willingness to take risks in the presentation of psychoanalytic theories to substructure his fiction, and a seriousness which has nothing to do with solemnity. The theme of personal liberation, which informs his major novels, is stated with urgency, and it is elaborated with imagination, and, very often, with great feeling. It is this theme, in my opinion, which makes his narratives so compelling. Finally, though he has remained unaffected by the developments over the last three decades in fictional techniques (as embodied in the writings of the "New Wave" in France, or of the "post-modernists" in Europe and America), his novels are always technically adroit and interesting in structure. He is not a writer easy to label, and this, ultimately, is his greatest achievement.

NOTES

[1] "Boys on the Elizabethan Stage: Influence upon the Drama," rev. of *Shakespeare's Boy Actors*, *The Times Literary Supplement*, 4 Feb. 1939, p. 74.

[2] Rev. of *Shakespeare's Boy Actors*, *The Quarterly Review*, 272 (April 1939), 370.

[3] Ken W. MacTaggart, "New Canadian Humorist," rev. of *The Diary of Samuel Marchbanks*, *The Globe and Mail*, 29 Nov. 1947, p. 9.

[4] Simon Paynter, rev. of *The Diary of Samuel Marchbanks*, *The Canadian Forum*, March 1948, p. 284.

[5] Vincent Tovell, rev. of *Fortune, My Foe*, in "Letters in Canada 1948: Drama," *University of Toronto Quarterly*, 18 (April 1949), 276.

[6] F. B. T., "Davies Play Needs Cast; 'Less Compact' as Book," rev. of *Fortune, My Foe*, *The London Free Press*, 19 Nov. 1949, p. 5.

[7] John A. Dewar, rev. of *Fortune, My Foe*, *The Canadian Forum*, Dec. 1949, p. 214.

[8] "This and That," rev. of *The Table Talk of Samuel Marchbanks*, *The Times Literary Supplement*, 10 Aug. 1951, p. 504.

[9] Vincent Tovell, rev. of *Eros at Breakfast and Other Plays*, in "Letters in Canada 1949: Drama," *University of Toronto Quarterly*, 19 (April 1950), 280.

[10] Herbert Whittaker, rev. of *At My Heart's Core*, *Theatre Canada*, I, No. 1 (Jan.–Feb. 1951), 16.

[11] Christopher Wood, "Davies' New Play," rev. of *At My Heart's Core*, *The Gazette* [Montreal], 16 Dec. 1950, p. 27.

[12] "Robertson Davies' First Novel Satirizes Little Theatre Folk," rev. of *Tempest-Tost*, *Toronto Daily Star*, 6 Oct. 1951, p. 27.

[13] B. K. Sandwell, "Civilized View of Canada," rev. of *Tempest-Tost*, *Saturday Night*, 27 Oct. 1951, p. 4.

[14] Jean-Charles Bonenfant, "Ballotés par la tempête," rev. de *Tempest-Tost*, *La Revue de l'Université Laval*, 6 (jan. 1952), 400–01.

[15] Claude Bissell, rev. of *Tempest-Tost*, in "Letters in Canada 1951: Fiction," *University of Toronto Quarterly*, 21 (April 1952), 265–66.

[16] Paul Bloomfield, rev. of *Tempest-Tost*, *The Manchester Guardian*, 4 July 1952, p. 4.

[17] "Beneath the Surface," rev. of *Tempest-Tost*, *The Times Literary Supplement*, 18 July 1952, p. 465.

[18] Nancy Lenkeith, "School-Play," rev. of *Tempest-Tost*, *The New York Times Book Review*, 13 July 1952, p. 17.

[19] Roy Kervin, "Tempest in Salterton," rev. of *Leaven of Malice*, *The Gazette* [Montreal], 25 Sept. 1954, p. 30.

[20] W. L. McGeary, "'Leaven of Malice' Hits Editor and College Don," rev. of *Leaven of Malice*, *Toronto Daily Star*, 25 Sept. 1954, p. 4.

[21] Eric Nicol, rev. of *Leaven of Malice*, *Vancouver Province*, 27 Nov. 1954, p. 15.

[22] Claude Bissell, rev. of *Leaven of Malice*, in "Letters in Canada 1954: Fiction," *University of Toronto Quarterly*, 24 (April 1955), 264, 266.

[23] John Metcalf, rev. of *Leaven of Malice*, *Spectator*, 4 March 1955, p. 266.

[24] Rev. of *Leaven of Malice*, *The New Yorker*, 3 Sept. 1955, p. 70.

[25] W. O'H., "New Davies Novel — Cinderella in London," rev. of *A Mixture of Frailties*, *The Montreal Star*, 16 Aug. 1958, p. 24.

[26] Mary Dunnett, "Human Follies and Frailties," rev. of *A Mixture of Frailties*, *The Globe and Mail*, 23 Aug. 1958, p. 9.

[27] Arnold Edinborough, "Enriched with Humanity," rev. of *A Mixture of Frailties*, *Saturday Night*, 13 Sept. 1958, pp. 29–31.

[28] Claude Bissell, rev. of *A Mixture of Frailties*, in "Letters in Canada 1958: Fiction," *University of Toronto Quarterly*, 28 (July 1959), 370.

[29] Rev. of *A Mixture of Frailties*, *The New Yorker*, 6 Sept. 1958, p. 119.

[30] Max Cosman, "The End of Reading," rev. of *A Voice from the Attic*, *The Commonweal*, 28 Oct. 1960, p. 135.

[31] Kerry McSweeney, rev. of *A Voice from the Attic*, *Queen's Quarterly*, 79 (Summer 1972), 286, 287.

[32] "Two Home-Grown Novels Come Highly Recommended," rev. of *Fifth Business*, *The Montreal Star*, 21 Nov. 1970, p. 21.

[33] Christopher Lehmann-Haupt, "A Magical Mystery Fiction," rev. of *Fifth Business*, *The New York Times*, 23 Nov. 1970, p. 35.

[34] L. J. Davis, "From Canada Comes a Master of the Novel," rev. of *Fifth Business*, *Book World*, 13 Dec. 1970, p. 1.

[35] Peter S. Prescott, "White Magic," rev. of *World of Wonders*, *Newsweek*, 22 March 1976, pp. 80–81.

[36] Ivon Owen, "The Salterton Novels," *The Tamarack Review*, No. 9 (Autumn 1958), p. 58.

[37] Owen, p. 63.

[38] Hugo McPherson, "The Mask of Satire: Character and Symbolic Pattern in Robertson Davies' Fiction," *Canadian Literature*, No. 4 (Spring 1960), pp. 18–30; rpt. in *Masks of Fiction: Canadian Critics on Canadian Prose*, ed. A. J. M. Smith, New Canadian Library Original, No. 2 (Toronto: McClelland and Stewart, 1961), p. 163. All further references to this work appear in the text.

[39] Hugo McPherson, "Fiction 1940–1960," in *Literary History of Canada: Canadian Literature in English*, 2nd ed., gen. ed. and introd. Carl F. Klinck (Toronto: Univ. of Toronto Press, 1976), II, 211, 215–17.

[40] Desmond Pacey, "Canadian Literature in the Fifties," in *Essays in Canadian Criticism 1938–1968* (Toronto: Ryerson, 1969), pp. 208–09.

[41] Gordon Roper, "Robertson Davies' *Fifth Business* and 'That Old

Fantastical Duke of Dark Corners, C. G. Jung,'" *Journal of Canadian Fiction*, 1, No. 1 (Winter 1972), 33–39; rpt. in *The Canadian Novel: Here and Now*, ed. John Moss (Toronto: NC, 1978), pp. 53–66.

[42] See Margaret Dyment, "Romantic Ore," *Journal of Canadian Fiction*, 2, No. 1 (Winter 1973), 83–84.

[43] Judith Skelton Grant, *Robertson Davies*, New Canadian Library, Canadian Writers Series, No. 17 (Toronto: McClelland and Stewart, 1978).

[44] David Monaghan, "'People in Prominent Positions': A Study of the Public Figure in the Deptford Trilogy," in *Studies in Robertson Davies' Deptford Trilogy*, ed. Robert G. Lawrence and Samuel L. Macey, English Literary Studies, Monograph Series, No. 20 (Victoria: Univ. of Victoria, 1980), p. 55.

[45] Elspeth Buitenhuis, *Robertson Davies*, Canadian Writers and Their Works (Toronto: Forum House, 1972).

[46] Patricia Morley, *Robertson Davies*, Profiles in Canadian Drama (Toronto: Gage, 1977).

[47] *Tempest-Tost* (1951; rpt. Markham, Ont.: Penguin, 1980), p. 13. All further references to this work appear in the text.

[48] See *Leaven of Malice* (1954; rpt. Markham, Ont.: Penguin, 1980), pp. 14–15, 64. All further references to this work appear in the text.

[49] *A Mixture of Frailties* (Toronto: Macmillan, 1958), p. 25. All further references to this work appear in the text.

[50] F. L. Radford, "The Apprentice Sorcerer: Davies' Salterton Trilogy," in Lawrence and Macey, eds., *Studies in Robertson Davies' Deptford Trilogy*, pp. 13–21.

[51] Robertson Davies, "The Deptford Trilogy in Retrospect," in Lawrence and Macey, eds., *Studies in Robertson Davies' Deptford Trilogy*, pp. 7–8. All further references to this work appear in the text.

[52] *Fifth Business* (Toronto: Macmillan, 1970), p. 9. All further references to this work appear in the text.

[53] F. L. Radford, "The Great Mother and the Boy: Jung, Davies, and *Fifth Business*," in Lawrence and Macey, eds., *Studies in Robertson Davies' Deptford Trilogy*, pp. 66–81.

[54] See Buitenhuis, *Robertson Davies*.

[55] *The Manticore* (Toronto: Macmillan, 1972), p. 119. All further references to this work appear in the text.

[56] C. G. Jung, *Memories, Dreams, Reflections*, ed. Aniela Jaffé, trans. Richard Winston and Clara Winston (New York: Vintage, 1965), p. 39.

SELECTED BIBLIOGRAPHY

Primary Sources

Davies, Robertson. *Shakespeare's Boy Actors*. London: Dent, 1939.

——. *Shakespeare for Young Players: A Junior Course*. Toronto: Clarke, Irwin, 1942.

——. *The Diary of Samuel Marchbanks*. Toronto: Clarke, Irwin, 1947.

——. *Overlaid: A Comedy*. Canadian Playwright Series. Toronto: Samuel French, 1948.

——. *Eros at Breakfast and Other Plays*. Toronto: Clarke, Irwin, 1949.

——. *Fortune, My Foe*. Toronto: Clarke, Irwin, 1949.

——. *The Table Talk of Samuel Marchbanks*. Toronto: Clarke, Irwin, 1949.

——. *At My Heart's Core*. Toronto: Clarke, Irwin, 1950.

——. *Tempest-Tost*. 1951; rpt. Markham, Ont.: Penguin, 1980.

——. *A Masque of Aesop*. Toronto: Clarke, Irwin, 1952.

——. *A Jig for the Gypsy*. Toronto: Clarke, Irwin, 1954.

——. *Leaven of Malice*. 1954; rpt. Markham, Ont.: Penguin, 1980.

——, and Tyrone Guthrie. *Renown at Stratford: A Record of the Shakespearean Festival in Canada 1953*. Toronto: Clarke, Irwin, 1954.

——, and Tyrone Guthrie. *Twice Have the Trumpets Sounded: A Record of the Stratford Shakespearean Festival in Canada 1954*. Toronto: Clarke, Irwin, 1954.

——, Tyrone Guthrie, Boyd Neel, and Tanya Moiseiwitsch. *Thrice the Brinded Cat Hath Mew'd: A Record of the Stratford Shakespearean Festival in Canada 1955*. Toronto: Clarke, Irwin, 1955.

——. *A Mixture of Frailties*. Toronto: MacMillan, 1958.

——. *A Voice from the Attic*. Toronto: McClelland and Stewart, 1960.

——. *A Masque of Mr. Punch*. Toronto. Oxford Univ. Press, 1963.

———, Arthur Murphy, Yves Thériault, W. O. Mitchell, and Eric Nicol. *Centennial Play*. Ottawa: Centennial Commission, 1967.

———. *Samuel Marchbanks' Almanac*. Toronto: McClelland and Stewart, 1967.

———. *Four Favourite Plays*. Toronto: Clarke, Irwin, 1968.

———. *The Voice of the People*. Searchlight, No. 304. Agincourt, Ont.: Book Society of Canada, 1968.

———, ed. *Feast of Stephen: An Anthology of Some of the Less Familiar Writings of Stephen Leacock*. Toronto: McClelland and Stewart, 1970.

———. *Fifth Business*. Toronto: Macmillan, 1970.

———. *Stephen Leacock*. New Canadian Library. Canadian Writers Series, No. 7. Toronto: McClelland and Stewart, 1970.

———. *What Do You See in the Mirror?* Searchlight, No. 218. Agincourt, Ont.: Book Society of Canada, 1970.

———. *Hunting Stuart and Other Plays*. Ed. Brian Parker. New Drama, No. 3. Toronto: new, 1972.

———. *The Manticore*. Toronto: Macmillan, 1972.

———. *Question Time*. Toronto: Macmillan, 1975.

———, Michael Booth, Richard Southern, Frederick Marker, and Lise-Lone Marker. *The Revels History of Drama in English, 1750–1880*. Vol. VI. London: Methuen, 1975.

———. *World of Wonders*. Toronto: Macmillan, 1975.

———. *One Half of Robertson Davies: Provocative Pronouncements on a Wide Range of Topics*. Toronto: Macmillan, 1977.

———. *The Enthusiasms of Robertson Davies*. Ed. Judith Skelton Grant. Toronto: McClelland and Stewart, 1979.

———. "The Deptford Trilogy in Retrospect." In *Studies in Robertson Davies' Deptford Trilogy*. Ed. Robert G. Lawrence and Samuel L. Macey. English Literary Studies. Monograph Series, No. 20. Victoria: Univ. of Victoria, 1980, pp. 7–12.

———. *The Rebel Angels*. Toronto: Macmillan, 1981.

———. *The Well-Tempered Critic: One Man's View of Theatre and Letters in Canada*. Ed. Judith Skelton Grant. Toronto: McClelland and Stewart, 1981.

———. *High Spirits*. Markham, Ont.: Penguin, 1982.

———. *The Mirror of Nature: The Alexander Lectures 1982*. Toronto: Univ. of Toronto Press, 1983.

Secondary Sources

"Beneath the Surface." Rev. of *Tempest-Tost*. *The Times Literary Supplement*, 18 July 1952, p. 465.

Bissell, Claude. Rev. of *Tempest-Tost*. In "Letters in Canada 1951: Fiction." *University of Toronto Quarterly*, 21 (April 1952), 265–66.

———. Rev. of *Leaven of Malice*. In "Letters in Canada 1954: Fiction." *University of Toronto Quarterly*, 24 (April 1955), 264–67.

———. Rev. of *A Mixture of Frailties*. In "Letters in Canada 1958: Fiction." *University of Toronto Quarterly*, 28 (July 1959), 370–71.

Bloomfield, Paul. Rev. of *Tempest-Tost*. *The Manchester Guardian*, 4 July 1952, p. 4.

Bonenfant, Jean-Charles. "Ballotés par la tempête." Rev. de *Tempest-Tost*. *La Revue de l'Université Laval*, 6 (jan. 1952), 400–01.

"Boys on the Elizabethan Stage: Influence upon the Drama." Rev. of *Shakespeare's Boy Actors*. *The Times Literary Supplement*, 4 Feb. 1939, p. 74.

Buitenhuis, Elspeth. *Robertson Davies*. Canadian Writers and Their Works. Toronto: Forum House, 1972.

Cosman, Max. "The End of Reading." Rev. of *A Voice from the Attic*. *The Commonweal*, 28 Oct. 1960, pp. 133–35.

Davis, L. J. "From Canada Comes a Master of the Novel." Rev. of *Fifth Business*. *Book World*, 13 Dec. 1970, p. 1.

Dean, John. "Magic and Mystery in Robertson Davies' Deptford Trilogy." *Waves*, 7, No. 1 (Fall 1978), 63–68.

Dewar, John A. Rev. of *Fortune, My Foe*. *The Canadian Forum*, Dec. 1949, p. 214.

Dunnett, Mary. "Human Follies and Frailties." Rev. of *A Mixture of Frailties*. *The Globe and Mail*, 23 Aug. 1958, p. 9.

Dyment, Margaret. "Romantic Ore." *Journal of Canadian Fiction*, 2, No. 1 (Winter 1973), 83–84.

Edinborough, Arnold. "Enriched with Humanity." Rev. of *A Mixture of Frailties*. *Saturday Night*, 13 Sept. 1958, pp. 29–31.

Gerson, Carole. "Dunstan Ramsay's Personal Mythology." *Essays on Canadian Writing*, No. 6 (Spring 1977), pp. 100–08.

Grant, Judith Skelton. *Robertson Davies*. New Canadian Library. Canadian Writers Series, No. 17. Toronto: McClelland and Stewart, 1978.

Heintzman, Ralph H. "The Virtues of Reverence." *Journal of Canadian Studies*, 12, No. 1 (Feb. 1977), 1–2, 92–95.

Keith, W. J. "*The Manticore*: Psychological and Fictional Technique." *Studies in Canadian Literature*, 3 (Winter 1978), 133–36.

Kervin, Roy. "Tempest in Salterton." Rev. of *Leaven of Malice*. *The Gazette* [Montreal], 25 Sept. 1954, p. 30.

Kirkwood, Hilda. "Robertson Davies." *The Canadian Forum*, June 1950, pp. 59–60.

Knelman, Martin. "The Masterful Actor Who Plays Robertson Davies." *Saturday Night*, June 1975, pp. 30–35.

Lawrence, Robert G. "A Survey of the Three Novels of Robertson Davies." *British Columbia Library Quarterly*, 32, No. 4 (April 1969), 3–9.

———, and Samuel L. Macey, eds. *Studies in Robertson Davies' Deptford Trilogy*. English Literary Studies. Monograph Series, No. 20. Victoria: Univ. of Victoria, 1980.

Lehmann-Haupt, Christopher. "A Magical Mystery Fiction." Rev. of *Fifth Business*. *The New York Times*, 23 Nov. 1970, p. 35.

Lenkeith, Nancy. "School-Play." Rev. of *Tempest-Tost*. *The New York Times Book Review*, 13 July 1952, p. 17.

MacTaggart, Ken W. "New Canadian Humorist." Rev. of *The Diary of Samuel Marchbanks*. *The Globe and Mail*, 29 Nov. 1947, p. 9.

McGeary, W. L. "'Leaven of Malice' Hits Editor and College Don." Rev. of *Leaven of Malice*. *Toronto Daily Star*, 25 Sept. 1954, p. 4.

McPherson, Hugo. "The Mask of Satire: Character and Symbolic Pattern in Robertson Davies' Fiction." *Canadian Literature*, No. 4 (Spring 1960), pp. 18–30. Rpt. in *Masks of Fiction: Canadian Critics on Canadian Prose*. Ed. A. J. M. Smith. New Canadian Library Original, No. 2. Toronto: McClelland and Stewart, 1961, pp. 162–75.

———. "Fiction 1940–1960." In *Literary History of Canada: Canadian Literature in English*. 2nd ed. Gen. ed. and introd. Carl F. Klinck. Toronto: Univ. of Toronto Press, 1976. II, 205–33.

McSweeney, Kerry. Rev. of *A Voice from the Attic*. *Queen's Quarterly*, 79 (Summer 1972), 284–87.

Metcalf, John. Rev. of *Leaven of Malice*. *Spectator*, 4 March 1955, p. 266.

Monk, Patricia. "Confessions of a Sorcerer's Apprentice: *World of Wonders* and the Deptford Trilogy of Robertson Davies." *Dalhousie Review*, 56 (Summer 1976), 366–72.

———. "Psychology and Myth in *The Manticore*." *Studies in Canadian Literature*, 2 (Winter 1977), 69–81.

————. *The Smaller Infinity: The Jungian Self in the Novels of Robertson Davies.* Toronto: Univ. of Toronto Press, 1982.

Morley, Patricia. "Davies' Salterton Trilogy: Where the Myth Touches Us." *Studies in Canadian Literature,* 1 (Winter 1976), 96–104.

————. *Robertson Davies.* Profiles in Canadian Drama. Toronto: Gage, 1977.

"The Myth and the Master." *Time* [Canada], 3 Nov. 1975, pp. 8–12.

Neufeld, James. "Structural Unity in 'The Deptford Trilogy': Robertson Davies as Egoist." *Journal of Canadian Studies,* 12, No. 1 (Feb. 1977), 68–74.

Nicol, Eric. Rev. of *Leaven of Malice. Vancouver Province,* 27 Nov. 1954, p. 15.

O'H., W. "New Davies Novel — Cinderella in London." Rev. of *A Mixture of Frailties. The Montreal Star,* 16 Aug. 1958, p. 24.

Owen, Ivon. "The Salterton Novels." *The Tamarack Review,* No. 9 (Autumn 1958), pp. 56–63.

Pacey, Desmond. *Creative Writing in Canada: A Short History of English-Canadian Literature.* Toronto: Ryerson, 1961, pp. 233–35, 256, 258–61, 266, 269, 272.

————. *Essays in Canadian Criticism 1938–1968.* Toronto: Ryerson, 1969, pp. 129, 208–09, 230, 239, 274–75, 280.

Paynter, Simon. Rev. of *The Diary of Samuel Marchbanks. The Canadian Forum,* March 1948, p. 284.

Prescott, Peter, S. "White Magic." Rev. of *World of Wonders. Newsweek,* 22 March 1976, pp. 80–81.

Radford, F. L. "Heinrich Heine, the Virgin and the Hummingbird: *Fifth Business* — A Novel and Its Subconscious." *English Studies in Canada,* 4 (Spring 1978), 95–110.

————. "The Apprentice Sorcerer: Davies' Salterton Trilogy" and "The Great Mother and the Boy: Jung, Davies, and *Fifth Business.*" In *Studies in Robertson Davies' Deptford Trilogy.* Ed. Robert G. Lawrence and Samuel L. Macey. English Literary Studies. Monograph Series, No. 20. Victoria, Univ. of Victoria, 1980, pp. 13–21, 66–81.

Rev. of *A Mixture of Frailties. The New Yorker,* 6 Sept. 1958, p. 119.

Rev. of *Leaven of Malice. The New Yorker,* 3 Sept. 1955, p. 70.

Rev. of *Shakespeare's Boy Actors. The Quarterly Review,* 272 (April 1939), 370.

"Robertson Davies' First Novel Satirizes Little Theatre Folk." Rev. of *Tempest-Tost. Toronto Daily Star,* 6 Oct. 1951, p. 27.

Roper, Gordon. "Robertson Davies' *Fifth Business* and 'That Old Fantastical Duke of Dark Corners, C. G. Jung.'" *Journal of Canadian Fiction*, 1, No. 1 (Winter 1972), 33–39. Rpt. in *The Canadian Novel: Here and Now*. Ed. John Moss. Toronto: NC, 1978, pp. 53–66.

Ryrie, John. "Robertson Davies: An Annotated Bibliography." In *The Annotated Bibliography of Canada's Major Authors*. Ed. Robert Lecker and Jack David. Vol. III. Downsview, Ont.: ECW, 1981, 57–279.

Sandwell, B. K. "Civilized View of Canada." Rev. of *Tempest-Tost*. *Saturday Night*, 27 Oct. 1951, pp. 4–5.

Sutherland, Ronald. "The Relevance of Robertson Davies." In *The New Hero: Essays in Comparative Quebec / Canadian Literature*. Toronto: Macmillan, 1977, pp. 73–83.

T., F. B. "Davies Play Needs Cast; 'Less Compact' as Book." Rev. of *Fortune, My Foe*. *The London Free Press*, 19 Nov. 1949, p. 5.

"This and That." Rev. of *The Table Talk of Samuel Marchbanks*. *The Times Literary Supplement*, 10 Aug. 1951, p. 504.

Thomas, Clara. "The Two Voices of *A Mixture of Frailties*." *Journal of Canadian Studies*, 12, No. 1 (Feb. 1977), 82–91.

Tovell, Vincent. Rev. of *Fortune, My Foe*. In "Letters in Canada 1948: Drama." *University of Toronto Quarterly*, 18 (April 1949), 276.

———. Rev. of *Eros at Breakfast and Other Plays*. In "Letters in Canada 1949: Drama." *University of Toronto Quarterly*, 19 (April 1950), 279–80.

"Two Home-Grown Novels Come Highly Recommended." Rev. of *Fifth Business*. *The Montreal Star*, 21 Nov. 1970, p. 21.

Warwick, Ellen. "The Transformation of Robertson Davies." *Journal of Canadian Fiction*, 3, No. 3 (Summer 1974), 46–51. Rpt. (revised) in *The Canadian Novel: Here and Now*. Ed. John Moss. Toronto: NC, 1978, pp. 67–78.

Whittaker, Herbert. Rev. of *At My Heart's Core*. *Theatre Canada*, 1, No. 1 (Jan.–Feb. 1951), 16–17.

Wood, Christopher. "Davies' New Play." Rev. of *At My Heart's Core*. *The Gazette* [Montreal], 16 Dec. 1950, p. 27.